Patterns

Politics and
in Bolivia

CW00970148

Patterns of Protest
Politics and Social Movements in Bolivia

John Crabtree

Latin America Bureau
LONDON

Patterns of Protest: Politics and Social Movements in Bolivia
was first published by
Latin America Bureau
1 Amwell Street
London EC1R 1UL
In 2005

Latin America Bureau is an independent research and
publishing organisation. It works to broaden public
understanding of human rights and social and economic
justice in Latin America and the Caribbean.

Editing: Jean McNeil
Cover design: Diseño Atlántico, Buenos Aires
Interior design and setting: Kate Kirkwood
Printed by Arrowsmith, Bristol
Cover image: Indymedia Argentina

A CIP catalogue record is available from the British
Library.

ISBN 1 899365 71 0

Contents

Prologue

Ana María Romero de Campero

Director of the Fundación UNIR Bolivia
First Defensora del Pueblo
(Ombudsman) de Bolivia

This book is indispensable for understanding what is going on in Bolivia today. John Crabtree has brilliantly managed to combine the tools and approach of the social researcher with those of the journalist to involve us in the shifting patterns of an as yet unfinished story. The synopsis of each of the cases under study is combined with the testimony of those who in one way or another have been involved as protagonists. At the same time, the analysis helps to explain not just the genesis of specific conflicts but the impact they have had – and continue to have – on the country.

A good deal of effort has been expended in Bolivia in seeking to understand the events described in this book, events which have helped to make recent years ones of considerable social agitation. But daily life sometimes overwhelms us and few authors up to now have managed to get beyond conjunctural analysis and subjective opinions. As an author and analyst John Crabtree has a distinct advantage; along with being well-versed in recent Bolivian history and having looked closely at the situations outlined in this book, he manages to view Bolivia from a certain distance.

His selection of case studies helps to set the scene and draw the characters of this drama. Here we have a vivid evocation of the road blockades on the Altiplano of September 2000; the eruption of Felipe Quispe as the standard bearer of an *indigenismo* nurtured on the past but demanding space in the present; and the charismatic figure of Evo Morales, leader of the coca farmers of the Chapare, and who has become a key political actor, one of the first pure-blooded indigenous Latin Americans with a chance of becoming president of his country. The actors are the multitudes involved in the water war in Cochabamba, who brought their own perspectives to the gas war in El Alto, and who took on the needs and concerns of the pensioners in the wake of the pension reform.

Each of the conflicts analysed here helps to explain how and why a country which won plaudits from the so-called 'international community' for its implementation of the neo-liberal model reacted so virulently when the effects on everyday life caused by this model became clear, when people saw how fundamental rights could be trampled underfoot in the name of the free market.

Oddly enough, the people who rose up over the last five years were often the very same who quietly suffered the adjustment policies that Víctor Paz Estenssoro introduced to put an end to the inflation that reached arithmetically dizzying heights in 1985. Anything, it seemed, was better than seeing the value of money simply evaporate, or taking whole suitcases of cash to the market to do the shopping. The now infamous Decree 21060, which ushered in the new economic, monetary and labour regime, justified the social cost of these measures, holding out the prospect of restored growth in return. This is the same promise uttered by one government after another in the years that followed. It has yet to be honoured.

Most analysts of Bolivian politics agree that two decades of democracy have not created political parties which satisfy people's expectations. This is particularly evident when we consider that since the fall of the Berlin Wall the left has found itself isolated on the global political map, and with it the *Central Obrera Boliviana* (Bolivian Workers' Confederation; COB). Those who pushed for market liberalisation did not encounter much resistance. The three parties that have pursued this objective in the last two decades – the *Movimiento Nacionalista*

Revolucionaria (Nationalist Revolutionary Movement; MNR), *Acción Democrática Nacionalista* (Nationalist Democratic Action; ADN) and the *Movimiento de la Izquierda Revolucionaria* (Movement of the Revolutionary Left; MIR) – won the support of 70% of the electorate by convincing voters that Bolivia could be a success story, improving its social indicators and its economic performance.

It would be wrong to say that nothing has been achieved. Some social indicators have improved, such as maternal and infant mortality rates and the numbers of children attending school. But the shortcomings are evident: poverty has increased; employment levels have collapsed; the informal sector has mushroomed; and more than a quarter of the population has been obliged to migrate, whether within the country or abroad.

The most recent Human Development Report from the United Nations Development Programme (UNDP) speaks to the consequences of all this. It shows that people have developed an enormous mistrust in both government and political parties. The reasons for this are fairly obvious. John Crabtree suggests that the party system collapsed because, among other things, there was no scope for policy apart from following recommendations from distant bureaucracies like the IMF and the World Bank. Corruption and impunity, along with the division of the spoils between the 'traditional' parties, only added to this loss of confidence. In spite of the many messages emanating from the population through protests and other mobilisations, political leaders appeared not to appreciate the extent of their own devaluation, at least until the general elections of 2002 and the municipal elections of 2004.

Patterns of Protest speaks about this and much more. It provides a full diagnosis of how people have become aware of their own power and have made use of the spaces provided by democracy to organise, to express their ideas, to vote, to elect, and to decide. The country's indigenous majority – 62%

according to the most recent census – has taken the decision to fight to claim its right to participate in decisions that affect it.

Those who hope for peaceful change look to the possible election of a Constituent Assembly in Bolivia. But there is no shortage of people who consider the conditions ripe for insurrection. This points to the need for a social pact that will provide conditions for peaceful coexistence and equal access to power. Those who believe that more social unrest is inevitable say that power has never been conceded peacefully or without a struggle. In this book John Crabtree provides valuable insight into contemporary Bolivian politics, and a better understanding of the context in which such changes might take place.

Introduction

For the best part of two weeks in October 2003, the citizens of El Alto, Bolivia, defied their government on the streets. Eventually they brought it down, forcing the unpopular president Gonzalo Sánchez de Lozada to resign and then flee to the United States. As people in this sprawling township daily manned makeshift blockades, they resisted repeated attempts by the army and police to dislodge them. They successfully cut the main access routes into the capital La Paz, placing an economic tourniquet around Bolivia's seat of government by blocking the entry of food and fuel. The uprising had started as a protest against new local tax administration procedures, but it rapidly developed into an all-out conflict against a government elected only sixteen months earlier and which had already lost any initial popularity it may have had. The mobilisation in El Alto came to be known as the 'gas war', since a key focus of public anger against the government was the plan to export Bolivian natural gas to the United States through Chile, the country's traditional enemy. While few at the outset had predicted that the protest would end in the ouster of the president and his government, it came to represent an important reaffirmation of 'people power' in Bolivian politics, and indeed in the rest of Latin America.

The term 'gas war' harked back to the so-called 'water war' in Cochabamba three years earlier. The success of the water war in forcing the then Banzer government to reverse its unpopular policies on water privatisation in Bolivia's third city encouraged a succession of protest movements in different parts of the country. These continued after the fall of Sánchez de Lozada, defying the authority of his successor, Carlos Mesa. The purpose of this book is to examine the various protest movements as they emerged during the Cochabamba water war and afterwards, to analyse both their particularities and what they had in common. In each case, it looks at the specific local characteristics that lay behind individual protest movements, their development and eventual outcomes.

The book seeks to give a voice to those who were involved, not only the leaders but others who took part. Before embarking on these individual stories it is worth asking a few broader questions as to why in recent years Bolivia – more so than most Latin American countries – has seen such a welling up of explosive social protest movements after a period of relative political stability. What is it that is so special about the country's political culture, with its lengthy tradition of protest and social mobilisation? What was the social impact of economic liberalisation from 1985 onwards, with respect to poverty, inequality and perceptions of social justice? How important was the lack of other more formal channels of political participation in contributing to a climate of protest? And how significant was outside interference in Bolivia's internal affairs in undercutting faith in the legitimacy of government? Answering these questions may help provide some clues as to why dissatisfaction built up to such a level during these years and expressed itself not through parliament or other formal channels, but on the streets.

A tradition of protest

Two traditions characterise Bolivia's political development since the time of Independence in the early 19th century. The first of these is a tradition of legalism and constitutionalism. The second is a tradition of mobilisation, frequently at the margins of the formally constituted political system. These two traditions overlap but have often worked in contradiction, helping to underscore the country's chronic political instability over much of the last two centuries. The tradition of mobilisation has involved both individual *caudillos* and social movements. In more recent times – at least since the Bolivian revolution of 1952 – the spirit of mobilisation has been kept alive mainly by the country's union confederation, the *Central Obrera Boliviana* (Bolivian Workers' Confederation; COB), and within it by the miners' federation, the *Federación Sindical de Trabajadores Mineros de Bolivia* (Union Federation of Bolivian Mineworkers; FSTMB). For decades, the miners provided the main nucleus of opposition to successive governments, using their industrial muscle in a country whose principle source of foreign exchange was tin. Although political parties of various colours played their part in the politics of the FSTMB and the COB, these institutions maintained their distance from government and the state, and for nearly 20 years after the 1964 coup the FSTMB and the COB were the main source of organised opposition to military rule.

The 1952 revolution and its aftermath

Between April 9th and the 11th 1952, a militia army with the support of the police overpowered government troops in La Paz, leading to the country's most important political change of the 20th century. Cheated out of his election victory the previous year, Víctor Paz Estenssoro returned from exile to become president. The revolution led to the nationalisation of the country's largest tin mines, owned previously by the so-called 'tin barons', the Patiño, Aramayo and Hochschild families. It also led to the abolition of serfdom, an agrarian reform and the introduction of universal franchise in elections. In the years that followed, the country was ruled by a succession of governments belonging to the *Movimiento Nacionalista Revolucionario* party (Nationalist Revolutionary Movement; MNR), led by Paz Estenssoro (1952-56),

Hernán Siles Zuazo (1956-60) and once again Paz Estenssoro (1960-64). During these years governments found themselves buffeted between the competing pressures of the United States and multilateral lending organisations on the one hand, and the country's powerful and radical labour movement on the other.

A coup in November 1964 ended the period of MNR hegemony and ushered in a period of military government that was to last on and off until 1982. General René Barrientos sought to cultivate social support for the new regime among the peasantry while repressing the labour movement, especially the miners. Between 1969 and 1971 there were two brief leftward-leaning military governments, led by General Alfredo Ovando (1969-70) and General Juan José Torres (1970-71). Under Ovando, the assets of Gulf Oil were nationalised. Torres was toppled by the right-wing Colonel Hugo Banzer Suarez (1971-78), who once again resorted to repression to control the labour movement. Under pressure from the Carter administration in Washington and with domestic unrest rising, Banzer was obliged to call elections in 1978. However, his attempts to secure the election of a military candidate backfired, leading to two years of struggle between the military and civilian politicians. The cycle of military regimes ended in 1982, following nearly two years in which officers closely connected with the drug mafias had vainly sought to hold onto power.

The closure in 1985 of most of Bolivia's nationalised mining operations, with the loss of 25,000 jobs, was a mortal blow to the FSTMB and gravely weakened the power of the COB. The collapse of world tin prices at the time (Bolivian underground mines were more expensive to run than open cast operations in countries like Brazil, Malaysia and Indonesia) coincided with the hyperinflation of the early 1980s, which the unions were powerless to prevent. The FSTMB's demise helped the consolidation of liberal economics in Bolivia, disarticulating its most virulent opponents. The closure of the mines changed the nature of Bolivian politics, weakening those contesting the state from outside and in their place helping to raise the profile of political parties and electoral politics. From the mid-1980s for 15 years or so the country enjoyed a period of unaccustomed political stability, ruled by a series of coalition governments based on pragmatic pacts between the main parties. Although there were frequent protests, these did not seriously challenge the new regime.

Bolivia remains a country with a strong civil society and a relatively weak state. Civil society had its roots in the communitarian traditions of Andean peasant society, with its long history of resistance to the encroachment of such 'western' values as private property, individualism and profit. In the past, these traditions have meshed with those of trade unionism (*sindicalismo*) with its powerful influence over organised sectors of the workforce. The crisis of the tin mining industry may have made it easier to install a liberal democracy after 1982, but it also had an important impact on civil society more generally. On the one hand, the mine closures led to the dispersal of mineworkers all over the country, and with them their political traditions and organisational experience. On the other, new sectors came to the fore to occupy the space left by the miners. They included the teachers and factory workers (*fabriles*), but those that made the biggest advance were the peasant unions. The formation in 1979 of a national peasant confederation, the *Confederación Sindical Unica de Trabajadores Campesinos de Bolivia* (Single Union Confederation of Bolivian Peasant Workers; CSUTCB), was a milestone, rejecting the ties of subordination that had linked peasants to the state since the 1953 agrarian reform. It was closely linked to the formation of a 'peasant' party, the *Movimiento Revolucionario Tupaj Katari* (Revolutionary Movement Tupaj Katari; MRTK).

The 1980s, therefore, brought a reorganisation of civil society, which not only became more complex and heterogenous but more representative of Bolivian society as a whole. This was also a time when the activities of non-governmental organisations

(NGOs) were proliferating, both in the rural and urban sphere, linked to the growth of new sources of funding from abroad. Bolivia today has thousands of grass-roots organisations, many of them community based. The density of such organisation varies a lot, but it is probably greatest in the rural Altiplano where age-old practices of reciprocity and collective action (notably through the *ayllu*) still prevail and where distrust of state-institutions and their policies is most marked. Nevertheless, community organisation has also developed rapidly in other parts of the country, such as in the lowland department of Santa Cruz, where the tradition of social organisation is much more recent.

These changes, along with others, such as the impact of urbanisation and the spread of education, have had the effect of changing traditions of mobilisation, not necessarily dissipating them. As will become clear, the tradition of *sindicalismo* lives on, often in a new guise, and suffused by other traditions such as ethnic or geographic affirmation. Collective identities and the determination to defend them remain strong, although it is clear that the weakened status of the COB means that it is no longer so able to defend or coordinate the activities of other social organisations as in the past.

The *ayllu* and the *sindicato*

Since the 1952 revolution, the main community institution in the rural world has been the *sindicato*. The 1953 agrarian reform led to the establishment of *sindicatos* in many rural areas. These were modelled on the mining and urban labour unions, and did not exist previously. Following the 1964 military coup they were co-opted by the military through the so-called Military-Peasant Pact (*Pacto Militar Campesino*). The establishment of the CSUTCB encouraged peasant unions to assert their independence from the state. Peasant unions have a dual representative role in expressing the political and commercial interests of peasant communities.

The *ayllu* has a much longer history, dating from pre-Columbian times. The *ayllus* constituted the basic micro-level unit of Andean society. Over the last 50 years, in spite of the spread of the *sindicatos*, the *ayllus* survived even in places close to urban centres. The role of the *ayllu* is to protect the territorial boundaries of the community, to decide on methods of production (including labour) and to provide governance. Traditional indigenous culture affords strong cultural bonds between the community and the land. The Law of Popular Participation (1994) officially recognised the *ayllu*, giving it a role that went beyond community affairs. In recent years, some Altiplano *sindicatos* have chosen to redefine themselves as *ayllus*.

Poverty, inequality and injustice

Bolivia remains South America's poorest country. National income per head of the population stood at around US$900 at the end of 2003, which means that Bolivia is rated internationally as a 'low-income' country. The only other Latin American countries where poverty rates are higher are Haiti and Nicaragua. According to the 2001 national census, the last available comprehensive survey of living conditions, nearly 60% of Bolivia's population is classified as 'poor'. Of that, roughly half is 'extremely poor' or 'indigent', with incomes of below the equivalent of US$1 a day. Only 16% of the population is believed to have sufficient income to cover basic needs. The geographical distribution of poverty is, however, quite striking. Extreme poverty is concentrated in rural areas of the western highlands, where very small-scale, usually subsistence peasant agriculture is the norm. The department with the most acute poverty is Potosí, where over 80% of the population was considered 'poor' in 2001; meanwhile in Santa Cruz, in eastern Bolivia, the figure was only 38%.

Socially as well as geographically, Bolivia is also among Latin America's most unequal countries. This at least is one of the conclusions of the World Bank, which in 2004 published an important study on inequality in the region. Inequality is more difficult to measure statistically than poverty. It depends a good deal on income and wealth levels among the most moneyed sectors of the population, and Bolivia's rich have never been too forthcoming about just how much they own or earn. But there is no doubting the huge disparities that exist between different social classes, between those of indigenous and non-indigenous origins, rural and urban, or between those from different parts of the country. Although it is difficult to point to an unerring relationship of cause and effect between economic policies and social outcomes, privatisation and other liberal policies appear to have increased that inequality; the rich have become richer over the last 20 years while poverty levels have barely changed. The World Bank is almost certainly right when it stresses the importance of ethnic factors in helping to explain the persistence of inequality in countries like Bolivia. Bolivia has a larger population of indigenous descent (62%) than any other Latin American country.

Barring miracles, there is little prospect of Bolivia meeting the UN Millennium Goal of halving the numbers of those living in poverty by 2015. According to the government's social and economic policy think-tank, the Bolivian economy needs to grow by around 7% per annum just to stop poverty rising. This is not just because the population is still growing quickly (though it is much slower than 20 years ago), but because the structure of the economy is such that the sectors that benefit from growth tend not to produce much by way of benefits for the poor. Bolivia's most dynamic growth sectors in recent years have been soya and natural gas, neither of which give rise to much employment and both benefit Bolivia's least-poor eastern region. The fastest annual growth rate since 1985 for the economy as a whole has been 5%.

Still more difficult to measure statistically, but arguably of even greater importance in terms of political behaviour, are perceptions of justice and fairness. There is a strong perception in Bolivia today that it is the wealthy and politically well-connected who have benefited most from the policies of economic liberalisation. With persistently high rates of unemployment and under-employment, the mass of poor people have seen no appreciable improvement in living standards, rather the reverse. It is the idea that liberalisation has served to propagate unfairness – borne out both by statistical observation as well as common sense – that has probably done more than anything else to undermine a sense of social cohesion and common interest. Added to this is the stark nature of ethnic differentiation and racial discrimination. Although the 1952 revolution removed the stigma of servile labour and recognised all as citizens, it did not put an end to discrimination. The class structure of Bolivia reflects its ethnic structure, with those of pure indigenous descent usually finding themselves at the bottom of the social pile. Still, Bolivia's indigenous peoples maintain their pride and social cohesion; increasingly they have come to demand respect as citizens.

Political parties and their critics

An important reason for the resurgence in street protest in Bolivia is the lack of faith of ordinary Bolivians in the institutions of formal democracy, particularly political parties. As in much of Latin America and indeed elsewhere, political parties are considered more part of the problem than the solution. Parties are seen not as vehicles of change but rather of social advancement on the part of their leaders, who prosper through corruption. Electoral promises are not usually taken very seriously. All opinion polls conducted over recent years point to the unpopularity of Bolivian political parties; they are seen as either corrupt or inept (or both). Still, compared with some other countries in the region, Bolivian political parties have proved remarkably durable in spite of this climate of mistrust. In large part, this is because – at least until 2004 – the only people who could legally participate in elections were those who were inscribed in officially registered parties. In 2004, the government changed the rules to enable those not on party lists to stand for electoral office.

We have seen how the establishment of a reasonably stable system of government in the late 1980s and 1990s owed much to the system of inter-party pacts and coalitions that propped up a series of governments. This was partly a consequence of Bolivia's unique electoral system which specifies that where no presidential candidate reaches an absolute majority of votes, the Congress (elected at the same time) chooses between the two front runners. With electoral support dispersed fairly evenly over a number of leading parties, no president since 1982 has received an overall majority of votes. All therefore have been elected as a result of alliances in Congress which then helped fashion post-electoral coalitions. Some of these alliances, such as that between the then centre-left *Movimiento de la Izquierda Revolucionaria* (Movement of the Revolutionary Left; MIR) and the right-wing *Acción Democrática Nacionalista* (Nationalist Democratic Action; ADN) in the 1989 elections that resulted in the MIR's Jaime Paz Zamora becoming president, seemed to sacrifice all ideological considerations on the altar of political expediency.

So while the system of pacts and coalitions helped build a degree of stability into the political system, it did so at the expense of political principles or any notion that parties might represent varying social sectors with different interests. Broadly speaking, the three main parties – the MNR, the MIR and the ADN – pursued similar policies from 1985 onwards, with any differences between them more apparent at election times than afterwards. This meant that they failed to fulfil one of the key functions that political parties are supposed to perform in a democracy, in providing the link between society (or the electorate) and the state (or government). Instead, their main interest appeared to be maximising their share in the carve-up of posts and positions, which in turn gave them access to government resources to benefit both themselves and their clienteles. In Bolivia this practice is known as *peguismo* (*pega* being slang for a job) or *cuoteo* (with each party enjoying its *cuota* of power). The system evolved from the late 1980s onwards, but it became particularly overt during the period of President Hugo Banzer's *megacoalición* (1997-2002) with the ADN, the MIR and a number of smaller parties vying for *pegas*. Subsequently, under the short-lived second Sánchez de Lozada government (2002-3), the main coalition partners – the MNR and the MIR – spent the best part of a year fighting one another for the plum jobs in state bureaucracy.

The awful reputation of the traditional parties and their leaders was evidently a major underlying reason for the October 2003 uprising in El Alto. These were widely seen as having failed to stand up for ordinary people's interests, while making large amounts of money from the public purse for their own benefit. It was therefore no accident that an independent, Carlos Mesa, who had been elected with Sánchez de Lozada on the MNR ticket in 2002, found some acceptance with the electorate as a substitute for Sánchez de Lozada following the latter's fall from grace. Indeed, this revulsion against traditional parties had already been clear 18 months earlier, at the time of the 2002 presidential and congressional elections, when two relatively new parties had burst upon the scene with strong grass-roots endorsement. The first was the *Movimiento Al Socialismo* (Movement Towards Socialism; MAS), a party led by the leader of the coca workers' movement of the Chapare, Evo Morales, and the second was the *Movimiento Indígena Pachakuti* (Pachakuti Indigenous Movement; MIP), led by the fiery Aymara nationalist Felipe Quispe. Between them, the MAS and the MIP won just over 27% of the vote, 8 (out of 27) Senate seats and 33 (out of 130) seats in the Chamber of Deputies. But even these 'anti-system' parties in time came to be seen as little different from their more traditional counterparts.

The *bloqueo*

The roadblock (*bloqueo*) has become the method of choice for direct action in the last twenty years, especially in rural areas. *Bloqueos* reflect the growing importance of peasants and rural communities as political actors. Because of the country's geography of relatively few major roads and the long distances between cities, a few strategically situated roadblocks can bring transport and commerce to a standstill. La Paz, with its few road links with the rest of the country, is particularly vulnerable. Where local communities are solidly behind a *bloqueo*, they can generally block roads faster than the police or military can clear them. Such situations can easily lead to violent outcomes.

Outside pressures

The way traditional political elites have been called into question also has had much to do with how they responded to outside actors more readily than to ordinary Bolivians. There has long been a strong nationalist tradition in Bolivian politics, something which reflects a history of outside intervention in the country's affairs. The country's geographical position in the heart of South America, its mineral wealth and the relative weakness of its state institutions have all enticed outsiders to involve themselves in its domestic politics. Bolivia has suffered territorially from the incursions of its neighbours – Antofagasta was taken by Chile in the War of the Pacific in 1879-1883, Acre by Brazil in 1903, and a large swathe of the Chaco by Paraguay in 1935. But it has been US involvement in Bolivia that has been most controversial, and US interference helps explain the levels of anti-US feeling that often surface in Bolivian politics.

The 1952 revolution, with its radical overtones of workers' control, raised the alarm in Washington, and in the 1950s successive US administrations went to great lengths to bring the revolution under control. As Cold War hysteria reached a climax, Bolivia appeared to represent a 'communist threat' in the Western Hemisphere. US funds were therefore made available on the condition that Bolivia limited its state intervention, sidelined the unions from mainstream politics and promoted the private sector. Economic assistance was directed towards the building up of privately-owned Santa Cruz agribusiness as a counterweight to the state-owned mining sector. The more radical actors who had taken part in the 1952 revolution were shunned; the 1964 presidential candidacy of Juan Lechín, the COB leader, was vetoed by Washington. During the era of military governments (1964-78), the United States kept Bolivia under tight control, although there were short periods in which the military exhibited nationalist leanings, for example the Ovando government (which nationalised Gulf Oil in 1969) and that of General Juan José Torres (1970-71).

As of around 1980, communism gave way to coca as the main concern of US policy toward Bolivia. As consumption of cocaine increased in the United States, Washington's economic assistance shifted to crop substitution, and in its pursuit of the 'war on drugs' the embassy in La Paz adopted at times an overtly interventionist stance. Bolivian political leaders were assessed according to their commitment on this score: Jaime Paz Zamora (president 1989-93) was denied a visa to enter the United States because of suspicions that he had links with the drugs trade. Pressure on the Bolivian government to eradicate coca in the country was probably at its most intense during the Banzer-Quiroga government (1997-2002), when the so-called Dignity Plan involved the militarisation of the Chapare region in Cochabamba. Perhaps not surprisingly, the plan encouraged resistance in the Chapare among those most virulently opposed to US intervention.

Since the 1980s, Bolivia has also come under strong pressure from the Washington-based multilateral financing agencies, chiefly the IMF, the World Bank and the Inter-American Development Bank (IDB), as well as bilateral donors. Bolivia's economic weakness has given these institutions enormous influence over economic policy and the design of the institutions to handle it. Again, such pressures were nothing new: in the 1950s and 1960s these agencies had played a determinant role in macroeconomic management, but after 1985 their role was no longer counterbalanced by political pressure from the union movement. But by the end of the 1990s the influence that the multilateral banks exercised over key areas of decision-making inevitably drew them into the political firing-line.

Unsurprisingly, foreign interventionism – mainly but not exclusively by the United States – became one of the factors that contributed to a questioning of Bolivian democracy in the 1990s. Bolivian governments, it seemed, were more beholden to pressure from outsiders than to the people who had elected them. The overt way in which US ambassadors intervened in the domestic arena to achieve policy outcomes favourable to Washington sometimes exposed governments and their officials to public ridicule. Similarly, the IMF's role in cajoling Bolivia towards meeting performance targets exposed the lack of autonomy of local officials in managing the economy.

Banzer, Sánchez de Lozada and Mesa

The 2002 elections proved to be a turning point in recent Bolivian history, ushering in a new phase of political confrontation. The period of relatively stable pacts between the three major parties – ADN, the MNR and the MIR – came to an end, and popular social forces gained a strong voice in Congress through the MAS and the MIP. It ended the second *Banzerato* (this time an elected government), although Banzer had been obliged to give up power the year before because of ill health. Narrowly won by Sánchez de Lozada for the MNR, the elections did not lead to a stable pact. Within 15 months, Sánchez de Lozada had been ousted, and the presidency went to his vice-president, Carlos Mesa. An independent journalist, Mesa sought to take advantage of the unpopularity of Bolivia's political parties. He defused the tensions created by Sánchez de Lozada over the government's energy policy by holding a referendum on the controversial issue of gas exports (see Chapter Six) and promising to convene a Constituent Assembly to revise the constitution and make the political system more responsive to grass-roots demands. By 2005 his initial popularity had waned, and he came under attack for his failure to resolve key pending problems. In March that year he found himself forced to threaten to resign to try to stem the tide of public protest. His term was due to end in 2007.

Voices of protest

The period that began with the Cochabamba water war and led up to the El Alto gas war represented a challenge to the shortcomings of electoral politics in Bolivia and, in a sense, a return to a more time-honoured way of expressing dissent. The relative political stability that began in the mid-1980s was broken, as people rediscovered the force of public protest. New political leaders emerged with the development of protest movements, and some old ones re-emerged. The pages that follow seek to explain the nature of these waves of protest: their causes, their evolution and their effects, paying particular attention to the variety of actors involved, the multiplicity of their agendas and their reflections on what protest meant to them.

1
The Cochabamba Water Wars

Compared with the arid, sun-scorched expanses of the Bolivian Altiplano, the usually verdant valley of Cochabamba can seem a promised land. Seen from the air, a criss-cross patchwork of green fields stretches out, divided up by hedges and trees. It appears a fruitful land, blessed by a moderate, almost Mediterranean, climate. *Cochabambinos* are proud of their climate, claiming theirs to be the land of 'eternal spring'. Situated at around 2,500 metres above sea level, Cochabamba is a pleasant mean between the intense humidity of the eastern lowlands and the equally intense aridity of La Paz and the rest of the Bolivian highlands. Agriculture has traditionally been the economic mainstay of the department. But despite the green fields, Cochabamba suffers from a chronic shortage of water, a shortage made manifest by rapid urban and population growth, as well as a long-standing lack of investment.

The use (or abuse) of water has long been a conflictive issue in the politics of the Cochabamba valley. There is a history of bitter and sometimes violent inter-communal clashes and disputes between different types of water users, urban versus rural. The growth of the city of Cochabamba (its population rose from 200,000 in 1976 to over 500,000 in 2001) plus the even faster growth of surrounding municipalities – like Sacaba, Vinto and Quillacollo – has added to water consumption rates. Together, the population of Cochabamba and its satellite towns stands at nearly 1 million. At times of rainfall shortage, this rapid urbanisation has led to fierce protests from farmers whose sources of supply have been drained by the use of deep wells to satisfy urban demand.

Water and its poor distribution is an issue frequently used by local politicians seeking to drum up support. Since the early years of the 20th century, there was never enough water to satisfy the needs of all users, and small-scale agriculturalists have been amongst those most at risk. It was for this reason that irrigation-dependant farmers developed community-based organisations to protect their interests. In 1970, for example, there was a major conflict in the township of Vinto, to the west of Cochabamba, over the proper distribution of water. But the response of drilling ever-deeper wells had the effect of further reducing the aquifer, and diminishing supplies for other users. More recently, in Tiquipaya, formerly an agricultural area that has been developed for luxury housing because land there was cheap, there have been bitter conflicts between farmers and the new residents over the use of water. The population of Tiquipaya has grown tenfold since 1976.

This problem of water shortage and the difficulties of managing an equitable distribution between different users helps explain the violent response to the Banzer government's scheme in 1999 to privatise Cochabamba's water supply. Existing users suddenly found themselves facing hugely increased charges for consumption of water, which most could ill-afford to pay. Users of irrigated water for agriculture found their water – a resource they had always believed was theirs as a gift of nature – suddenly appropriated by a foreign multi-national. The organisations that had developed over the years to defend ancestral rights – known in Bolivia as *usos y costumbres* – were suddenly deployed in the fight against water privatisation. They joined forces for the first time with other users, mainly urban, and with the *cocaleros* (coca farmers) of the Chapare (see Chapter Two), in what turned into a lengthy, bitter, violent but ultimately successful campaign to force the government to retreat.

Privatisation a la Boliviana

As in other countries in Latin America, debt-related structural adjustment involved shifting resources from the public to the private sector. From the 1952 revolution onwards, the public sector had assumed a central role in the model of national development. Cuba apart, Bolivia had one of the most state-dominated economies of any country in Latin America. The debt crisis of the early 1980s changed all that. It exposed the financial weakness of the state and gave its creditors (especially the multilateral banks) a pivotal role in the design of policy. The experience of hyperinflation during the left-wing government of Hernán Siles Zuazo (1982-85) dramatised the need for fresh policies to deal with Bolivia's structural economic problems, and particularly the bankruptcy of its government. The first and one of the most dramatic moves in the direction of reducing state involvement in the economy was the decision in 1985 of the new Paz Estenssoro government to close down most of the operations of the state-run *Corporación Minera de Bolivia* (Bolivian Mining Corporation; Comibol). The summary closure of the country's largest mines, nationalised in 1952, saw the cutting of more than 25,000 mineworkers from the public sector payroll. This gave a new prominence to the country's privately owned mining sector, a major player in which was the family of Gonzalo Sánchez de Lozada, Paz Estenssoro's planning minister and a key architect of the policies of structural adjustment.

It was under the presidency of Sánchez de Lozada (1993-97) that privatisation became a major plank of policy. Although the previous government of Jaime Paz Zamora (1989-93) had taken some preliminary steps in this direction, Sánchez de Lozada resolved to sell off all Bolivia's major public companies to private investors. He promised that this would release entrepreneurial skills and money to generate employment and bring other benefits for all Bolivians. Indeed, in his manifesto – the so-called *Plan de Todos* – Sánchez de Lozada laid great emphasis on the need to use privatisation as a tool to achieve the sort of social benefits that would in turn help build political support for liberal policies. The system that he devised was known as 'capitalisation', by which the state would offer 50% of the ownership of specific public companies along with unfettered management control. The other 50% of the shares would be held in a trust fund, to be administered by private pension funds on behalf of the Bolivian public, the income being used to finance a programme of universal old age pensions. This pension entitlement became known as the Bonosol. The term capitalisation was partly adopted for political reasons; Sánchez de Lozada knew that privatisation had become a dirty word elsewhere in Latin America and that it would be a particularly hard sell in Bolivia. Capitalisation also had the advantages of enabling capital to be brought in quickly and had a social justification in the shape of the Bonosol (see Chapter Four).

The first company to come under the capitalisation hammer was the *Empresa Nacional de Electricidad* (National Electricity Company; ENDE), responsible for around two-thirds of Bolivia's electricity generation, distribution and transmission. It was divided up into smaller units, and then sold mainly to foreign buyers. The government had intended the telecommunications company Entel to be the first sale, but it changed its mind because of opposition among the unions in the industry. It was eventually sold at a higher price than anticipated to Stet of Italy. Then came Lloyd Aéreo Boliviano (LAB), the 75-year old flag carrier, for which there was only one offer, from Brazil's Sao Paulo-based VASP airline. It was opposed by the company's workforce as well as regional groupings which feared that privatisation would mean axing non-profitable routes that had been maintained for social and political reasons. Following LAB came the *Empresa Nacional de Ferrocarriles* (National Railway Company; ENFE), the run-down state railways with its two disconnected networks, one in the Altiplano and the other centred on Santa Cruz. Among huge protests from the workforce and other opponents of privatisation, ENFE was sold for a paltry 13 million dollars to a Chilean firm, Cruz Blanca. Last, but by no means least, was *Yacimientos Petrolíferos Fiscales Bolivianos* (Bolivian National Oil Company; YPFB), the jewel in Sánchez de Lozada's capitalisation crown. This sold for 835 million dollars, about the same as all the rest of the capitalisations together, to a number of different international oil/gas concerns, including Enron, Shell, Amoco and an Argentine consortium. Capitalisation also brought changes to the legal framework in each sector and the creation of new regulatory agencies to protect the public interest.

Predictably, the sell-off of these companies prompted street protests and plentiful criticism in the media. Among the most virulent opponents were the workers of the various companies concerned who feared that privatisation would lead to mass redundancies. In most cases, the government sought to buy off such opposition by offering workers special shares in the new companies. Overall, however, Sánchez de Lozada did not find himself swamped by public protests, and his government won political plaudits for its other social programmes, such as *Participación Popular*, its education reforms and the Bonosol. Plus, as we have seen, the economic and social stresses caused by hyperinflation in the early 1980s had weakened the union movement and reduced its capacity to mobilise public protest.

Water privatisation in Cochabamba was a different story. The Banzer government decided in 1999 to sell off the Cochabamba water distribution system, previously run by a municipal entity called Semapa, to International Water, a subsidiary of Bechtel, the US multinational, in the guise of a new company called Aguas del Tunari. This generated massive controversy. The law that facilitated the sale (Law 2029) was passed by stealth with a minimum of public consultation with affected parties. It was rushed through Congress at break-neck speed to avoid discussion and publicity. As well as the obvious problem of privatising something basic to human health, it was assumed at the time that this sense of urgency owed much to pressures from the World Bank, which had long been cajoling Bolivia into putting its water and sewerage operations in private hands. The lack of transparency or consultation may also have reflected the fairly murky provenance of International Water, a Cayman Islands-registered company about which little was known. The degree of independence of the new system of water regulation, ostensibly there to protect the public interest, inspired little confidence among consumers. The final straw, and the factor that triggered months of disturbances, was the announcement just weeks after the 1999 local elections that Aguas del Tunari was raising water tariffs for urban consumers by between 100% and 300% and offering nothing in return by way of promised new investments. The recently re-elected mayor of Cocha-bamba, Manfred Reyes Villa, a close ally of President Hugo Banzer, had made no mention of such an increase in his election campaign.

The whole saga of water privatisation in Cochabamba was also connected with a number of rival schemes, supported by different parties and interest groups, designed to 'resolve' the city's longstanding water supply problems once and for all. As is often the case in Bolivian politics, these interest groups had a material interest in the different projects on offer. "Their main aim was to make money quickly," says Fernando Salazar, who has studied the history of water projects in Cochabamba. "Public policy was not public at all." The most ambitious scheme, backed by Banzer and his allies in the 1997 elections, and afterwards in his *megacoalición* (which included Reyes Villa), was the Misicuni project, a water and hydro scheme in the mountains to the north-west of Cochabamba. Under construction for years, the Misicuni project has yet to add a litre of water to Cochabamba's supply and probably won't for years to come. According to Salazar, it has been a long tale of corruption and huge cost over-runs. An alternative scheme, touted by the MNR and its allies at the time of the 1997 elections, was the Corani project, involving the piping of water to the city from the Corani reservoir, north-east of Cochabamba. The advantages of this over Misicuni was that it would be cheaper and quicker to construct, but the contracts were less lucrative and the scheme failed to find favour with the Banzer government.

Anatomy of the protest

Popular mobilisation in and around Cochabamba began in November 1999 with the blockage of roads throughout the department, initially just for a 24 hour period. Protestors blocked all three of the main arteries leading into Cochabamba: in the township of Sacaba to the north on the main road to Santa Cruz through the Chapare; in the Valle Alto to the south-east on the old road to Santa Cruz and out towards Sucre; and at several points on the main road running west towards Oruro and La Paz. Sporadic protests continued throughout the month and on into December, when urban workers organised demonstrations. It was in December that an umbrella organisation, the *Coordinadora del Agua*, was established to coordinate actions throughout the department. Intermittent negotiations with the government continued in January 2000, despite bouts of severe police repression, but it was in February that the confrontation came to a climax. On February 4th, there was a massive march from the four points of the compass towards the city's main square, bringing together the various different sectors that opposed the Aguas del Tunari concession. Of the scores of thousands taking part, hundreds of people were wounded in pitched battles on the city's streets, with special riot police being drafted in from La Paz.

Voices: The *Coordinadora*

Oscar Olivera is a leader of the *Federación Departamental de Fabriles* (factory workers), but also he was the leader of the *Coordinadora del Agua*, and more recently of the *Coordinadora del Gas* (see Chapter Six). His office is up two flights of rickety stairs, just around the corner from the main square in Cochabamba. The building also houses the *Central Obrera Departmental* (Departmental Workers' Confederation; COD). It has a fine view over the leafy plaza, and traditionally this is the point where demonstrations in the city come together.

There was an accumulation of public outrage during 1999 and 2000. People felt wholly alienated from the way in which decisions were being made by just a small bunch of people. The water issue brought us together, because water has been scarce here for 50 years. The political class here is short-sighted and corrupt. The increase in water tariffs would have absorbed about one-fifth of the income of many people in the city. For the campesinos *it represented the appropriation of a resource which they had always used. The* regantes *[farmers of irrigated land] were the prime movers. They had their own forms of organisation and for them water belonged to the community; it couldn't just be privately owned or managed. The mobilisation over water brought together city and country, man and woman, informal worker and formal. It was something completely new. It made people aware of the nature of the economic model. What people want is social justice, respect and health.*

With the water war, people recovered their voice. The issue of natural resources is fundamental in bringing people together. They took the decisions, since there was no caudillo *out in front. It was a big victory. Water was not privatised in the end, and Bechtel was kicked out. But more importantly, people became aware that it was possible to get bad policies changed. If there had been no victory in the water war, there would never have been a gas war.*

But we have to be like water itself: transparent and always moving forward. The regantes *provide a good example of how to organise. Unlike many* sindicatos*, they are participative and open in the way they operate.*

The scale of the violence further alienated public opinion against the water privatisation law. "The whole of Cochabamba was lined up in opposition to Aguas del Tunari," says one foreign observer present at the time. The final 'battle' of the Cochabamba water war took place on April 4th, 10 weeks after Manfred Reyes had withdrawn the *Nueva Fuerza Republicana* (New Republican Force Party; NFR) from the ruling government coalition. It coincided with protests in other parts of the country, notably on the Altiplano. Once again, there was a coordinated round of roadblocks, but with far more *bloqueos* than before. For instance, on the road northwards to the Chapare the *cocaleros* erected blockages every few kilometres for a distance of up to 200 kilometres from Cochabamba. Within the city itself, the main civic and union organisations declared a strike which, in conjunction with the road blocks, brought economic life to a halt. The public order situation was rapidly getting out of control. The declaration of a 'state of siege' and the sending in of army reinforcements did nothing to calm things down, and eventually – having refused to enter into a dialogue with the Coordinadora because it lacked official status (*personaría jurídica*) – Banzer decided to climb down. The government ended up rescinding the contract with Aguas del Tunari and revoking Law 2029.

A signal characteristic of all these mobilisations was the heterogeneity of their social make-up. They involved a broad front of sectors and organisations representing almost all shades of opinion in and around the city, surrounding farming areas and places further away like the Chapare and the Upper Valleys (*Valles Altos*). The initial impetus has come chiefly from the *regantes*, for whom the idea of private ownership of water resources by others was anathema. Fighting for water resources was nothing new for these farmers, whose local organisations were geared up to taking on those who habitually stole community water. Water was widely regarded as a gift of nature, vouchsafed by inheritance, tradition and even God. The defence of *usos y costumbres* therefore had both an economic, social and cultural logic. When it became known that the Law 2029 envisaged the appropriation of water sources, both surface and subterranean, in addition to all the wells that people had sunk at their own expense, it produced an instant and explosive reaction. But the campaign of the *regantes* to overturn the law quickly gained a wider significance, leading to the formation of the *Coordinadora del Agua* in December 1999.

Voices: The *regantes*

Mallco Rancho is a small farming community in the district of Sipe Sipe, to the west of Cochabamba. It produces vegetables for the urban market, chiefly onions and carrots, but also alfalfa for cattle feed. It relies entirely on irrigation through a system of surface channels and bore holes that use mechanical pumps. Since the water war, people in Mallco Rancho are very jumpy about outsiders taking away their water supply. As we walked past one of the pumps and asked to photograph it, our guide warned us to keep clear. "They'll think you're from Semapa or the World Bank," he told us, "the last time I came here with some Dutch university students, they were very nearly pelted with stones."

Don Juan Saavedra, who was nearly 90 when we met him, is a revered figure in Mallco Rancho. For nearly thirty years he was the *juez del agua* (water judge) for the valley of the Viloma river. This is an important position, involving regulation of the available water to members of the various communities in the valley. It also involves defending the community's interests when outsiders threaten to appropriate their water supply. In his house, he keeps records of community control over water that go back to the 1930s.

Each community has someone whose job it is to regulate the use of water. In my time it was never a big problem, since everyone respected the usos y costumbres. *Now there's a lot of theft, and the water doesn't reach everyone. We need much more water than before. When I was younger I was* mayordomo *(foreman) on an estate, so I know how to regulate things. Here we don't need water metres to regulate flows, we do it by eye.*

Back in 2000, the leaders of the community decided to take part in the protests, because the government threatened to take our water away and give it to other people. Without water you cannot live. So we all manned the road blocks, taking it in turns. Some even slept by the roadside. Then we marched to Cochabamba.

The water vigilance committee meets on the twentieth of the month as regular as clockwork. The Misicuni project would probably benefit us, but then Cochabamba would take most of the water. What we need is a small dam upstream on the River Viloma. Between us, we paid US$13,000 for a 150 metre well and a water pump. We're still paying it off, with help from relatives of the community living abroad. They wanted to take this from us. Are you surprised that we protested?

The urban dimension of the water war also became clearer by the end of 1999, as consumers absorbed the impact of the tariff increases announced earlier in December by Aguas del Tunari. Urban protest was given leadership by the COD, especially the *fabriles* who are among the prime movers of the COD in Cochabamba. However, it involved other sectors as well. Chief among them were the residents of low-income townships on the outer fringes of the city to the south. Although most of these lacked piped water in their homes and therefore were not directly affected by the sudden price increases announced by Aguas del Tunari, any increase in the mains supply would raise the cost of water sold in these neighbourhoods by water tankers. These communities had long aspired to access the mains system because those connected to the Semapa water network paid far less for the water they consumed than those dependent on (often unscrupulous) water traders with their tanker trucks. Strong neighbourhood committees had striven for this objective, making water a key issue in the politics of the neighbourhood. A study conducted by the university in Cochabamba in these southern districts concluded that 98% of those interviewed took part in one way or another. "People got involved in the water wars because they wanted access to the Semapa network," says one of the researchers involved.

Voices: Slum-dwellers in Cochabamba

Father Luis Sánchez is a Jesuit priest from Barcelona. He lives and works in the southern district of Cochabamba, the poorest part of the city where most people still lack piped water in their homes. The neighbourhood is called *Villa Hermosa* (Beautiful Town), but hardly lives up to its name. Most of those living here have migrated since the mid-1980s. They have come from all over Bolivia, ex-miners from Potosí, Quechua speakers from Chuquisaca, Aymaras from La Paz and Oruro. Many of the more recent arrivals live in homes of adobe with corrugated iron roofs perched precariously on steep hillsides. The Centro Vicente Cañas, run by the Catholic Church, offers practical advice on a variety of matters. Amongst other things, Padre Luis heads up the Permanent Assembly on Human Rights (APDH). And after 2000 until he stepped down in 2004, he was also on the board of Semapa, representing consumers in the southern slums of the city.

The main thing that mobilised people here was the expropriation of all sources of water in the community. Around half of the people live from wells that they themselves had sunk. In most neighbourhoods there are neighbourhood water committees. Most wells are about 80 metres deep, and of those a large proportion produce salty water that's not very good for drinking. The committees are in charge of distributing water.

All of a sudden, it became illegal to have these sources of water. People would end up having to pay for water from sources in which they themselves had invested their meagre earnings. Whole neighbourhoods therefore were mobilised. This was the fundamental issue. Also, the idea of privatisation doesn't square with the way people think about water. Most people who live here are of campesino origin, and have quite traditional ways of organising themselves and their communities. People have learned a lot about water management over the years; it's not so easy to pull the wool over their eyes.

By the end of 1999, a coalition of interests had emerged on the water issue. This involved a wide spectrum of the local population, though the unity of purpose was frequently tested by divisions and squabbles between rival leaders. The city's neighbourhood associations, mainly controlled by Manfred Reyes and his NFR party, began to break ranks with the government at this point. Similarly, the influential *Comité Cívico*, representing local business interests, gave its backing. The *cocaleros* from the Chapare, a mere three hours away from Cochabamba by road, gave their support, enabling the strategically important highway to Santa Cruz to be blocked. Reacting against the violent tactics used by the government and threatened by the large tariff increases, middle class residents also joined in. Even the Catholic Church, which acted as mediator, unofficially gave its blessing to the protestors. "You saw *monjitas* (nuns) running to protect marchers from tear gas and the batons," said a foreign aid worker in the city. It was the breadth of this alliance, its capacity to integrate actors in both rural and urban communities and from different social strata that, despite problems of coordination, gave it its strength. Yet this was a spontaneous movement with a dynamic of its own, not the result of any pre-meditated political strategy. "We had no idea of the significance of all this," comments one close observer. "We never really dreamt that we would have the power to drive out a multinational, the power to force the government to rescind its legislation. In the end we were all amazed by what we achieved."

The story since 2000

In the wake of the Cochabamba water wars, responsibility for water management in the city and surrounding areas was returned to Semapa, where it had begun. Briefly, Semapa was administered by the *Coordinadora del Agua*, until a new board of directors was appointed. The president of Semapa is appointed by the mayor's office in Cochabamba, which means that until the 2004 mayoral elections (won in Cochabamba by a rebel from NFR) the position had been the gift of that party. However, Semapa's board of directors also includes people elected by the users. It is for this reason that Padre Luis, along with Raúl Salvatierra, in the southern sector of the city became members. And, as they are at pains to point out, victory in the water war has not brought any final resolution of the problems facing water users, whether rural or urban. Due to the number of people illegally tapping into the mains system and the loss of water through seepage from ancient pipes, Semapa loses around 55% of the water that enters its system. Major investment is needed to reduce this.

With the Misicuni project still far from completion and Corani effectively shelved, water shortage is still as acute as ever. The response of Semapa has been to fall back on the practice of drilling ever deeper wells in the hope of tapping underground sources of water. Not only is this a costly, hit-and-miss business, but it tends to further deplete the aquifer at the expense of those dependent on surface water and shallower bore holes. Partly as a result of the efforts of Padre Luis and his friends, some progress has been made in the poorest neighbourhoods in the south in extending the Semapa network to households previously reliant on water tankers, but still over half the households lack access to tapped water. According to Luis, "there have been lots of projects and promises from Semapa, but not much to show for them." The *regantes* of Sipe Sipe still accuse villagers nearby of stealing their water, meanwhile residents in nearby Vinto openly admit to siphoning off mains water illegally to meet their water needs.

The financial plight of Semapa, derived partly from lack of working capital but also from management problems, is such that it is unable to use available sources of finance for water and sewerage schemes. In 2004, for example, there was the possibility of borrowing $2 million from the Andean Development

Corporation, but Semapa's debt situation prevented it from making use of these funds. At a deeper level, the future management of Cochabamba's water supply system faces an almost philosophical divide. While those capable of providing the necessary finance, such as the World Bank and the IDB, would prefer a private-sector, businesslike approach to water management, the users of the system want their voice to be heard and want a participatory role in management. Many users (especially those living in rural areas) still find the notion of having to pay for water unacceptable. Much, therefore, revolves around the contentious issues of pricing and ownership.

This raises in turn the issue of inequality of access and discrimination in the cost of water between different users. Those worst off are people without tapped water, who depend on the water tankers for their supply. They pay up to 10% of their household income on buying water, whereas elsewhere in the city the average is nearer 1%. However, they consume much less water. Average per capita consumption in Cochabamba is five times higher than in areas where there is no piped supply, where a family would have to make do with as little as 20 litres a day. In wealthier neighbourhoods, people use sprinklers on their lawns without a thought for problems of supply. Carmen Ledo, a leading water expert at the San Simón University, has undertaken studies of water consumption in poor neighbourhoods, and concludes that Semapa needs to introduce a differentiated tariff that charges rich neighbourhoods more and poor neighbourhoods less for the water they consume. "In the northern suburbs, middle class families pay very little for excellent water provision, and this just encourages waste," she says. Rather than study poor areas and their water needs, she advocates measuring water consumption in rich neighbourhoods: "The contrast would really make the point of underlining social inequalities."

Impact of the water war

Beyond the still unresolved local problems of water supply management, the importance of the Cochabamba water war lies in how it showed that it was possible to resist the tide of privatisation. 1999-2000 proved in many ways to be a turning point. As Oscar Olivera pointed out, without the Cochabamba water wars, the mobilisation against the export of gas would have been unthinkable. Almost for the first time since 1985, when economic liberalisation was initiated under Paz Estenssoro, ordinary people registered their opposition to the policies on offer, finding common cause against a perceived external enemy. The water war also had the effect of pushing up the agenda the issue of managing natural resources on behalf of those dependent on them for their livelihood and exposing double standards in government rhetoric about the need for participation.

However, the situation in Cochabamba was to some degree special, and this helps explain why water privatisation was so controversial in Cochabamba, when in La Paz it met with less opposition. The history of water shortage in Cochabamba and the sort of organisation to which it gave rise is one reason. Another was the extraordinarily inept way in which privatisation was conducted. Not only did it preclude any attempt to involve people, but it led to a price shock that took even wealthy consumers aback. The government's resorting to heavy-handed violence and repression in its bid to intimidate its opponents and reassert political control only made things worse.

For the popular opposition to the Banzer government, the water wars were an unexpected victory, one that arose from a movement that had emerged spontaneously in response to events as they unfolded and which ended up commanding almost universal support. Says Olivera, "when we kicked out Bechtel we had no idea how significant the whole thing would turn out to be." For opponents of globalisation worldwide, events in Cochabamba were followed with interest. At the 2002 World Summit in Johannesburg, Cochabamba was held up as a blueprint of what could be done when the people confront policies by taking matters into their own hands.

For the foreign investment community, however, Cochabamba was an ominous sign, heralding further attempts to reverse the privatisation agenda of Sánchez de Lozada. In 2004 and 2005, President Carlos Mesa was to come under strong pressure to renationalise the oil and gas industry rather than simply change the way foreign companies were taxed. At the beginning of 2005, following major disturbances in El Alto, Mesa was eventually obliged to rescind the contract with Aguas de Illimani to provide water and sewerage in La Paz and El Alto. According to its critics, Aguas de Illimani (a company belonging to Suez Lyonnais des Eaux of France) was charging excessive amounts for connection to the mains supply for people living on the fringes of El Alto.

2
Coca and the *Cocaleros*

A triumphal arch erected by the local authorities and in need of a little paint greets the visitor to Villa Tunari, proclaiming it to be the capital of 'ethno-eco-tourism'. There is no mention here of Villa Tunari's main claim to fame over the last decades as the gateway to Bolivia's coca country. It is a steamy place situated at the end of the long descent from Cochabamba, where the mountains meet the tropical lowlands that stretch northwards and eastwards into Amazonia. It is perched on a strip of land, with rivers on either side. This gives it a strategic importance, since there are two bridges in swift succession before the road continues eastwards into the Chapare proper and then on to Santa Cruz. It is the control point for everyone entering or leaving the Chapare.

Villa Tunari, like other towns in the Chapare region, has grown rapidly in recent years. Twenty-five years ago it was just a small village, an outpost of officialdom before you entered the Chapare proper, a region where coca was king. It had one small hotel, a couple of brothels, a few houses and the outpost of UMOPAR (*Unidad Móvil de Patrullaje Rural*), the militarised US-funded Bolivian anti-drug squad. Today it has grown into a thriving town, sporting at least a dozen hotels, several restaurants and a variety of government offices. It is also the local headquarters of the US Agency for International Development (USAID), as well as the European Union's and the Spanish government's anti-narcotics 'alternative development' efforts.

The growth of Villa Tunari over this time owes everything to the coca boom in the Chapare since the 1970s and the attempts of a succession of governments (under strong US pressure) to counter it. The presence of agencies like the Ombudsman's Office (*Defensoría del Pueblo*) and CASDEL, a human rights protection team, is evidence that the struggle to eradicate coca has been violent and costly in terms of rights violations. If you want to be sure of a room in one of the town's hotels you had better book well in advance; most rooms are occupied by anti-drug 'advisors' or foreign contractors of one sort or another.

The road to Villa Tunari from Cochabamba, which first led to the opening up of the area for colonisation by poor migrants from the Bolivian highlands, was built in the 1960s under the US assistance programme to Bolivia. No-one at the time anticipated that within a few years the Chapare would become one of the world's major sources of coca, the raw material for cocaine. Since then the road has been extended through the Chapare, linking up with Santa Cruz. It is now the main route linking the east and west of the country, a key economic artery, adding to the commercial importance of Villa Tunari. This also gives it a strategic importance when it comes to organising road blocks. The road to Santa Cruz stretches off in an easterly direction, passing through a number of other once small settlements that have mushroomed into medium-sized towns in recent years: Shinahota, Chimore, Ivergarzama and others. Each have become centres for the different *federaciones* (federations) to which the *cocaleros* belong. It is the *federaciones* that have become the main target of government efforts to eradicate coca.

Coca eradication and its impact

Although coca has been grown in Bolivia since time immemorial and was a much prized commodity in pre-Columbian times, it was only in the 1970s that it took off as a major export crop. Traditionally, the main area of coca cultivation has been

in the Yungas, steep sided, semi-tropical valleys that lead down
from the cordillera towards the jungle lowlands in the department of La Paz. But the 1970s saw the development of the
Chapare in Cochabamba and adjoining parts of Santa Cruz as
the main growing area for export coca. It was an area of tropical forests with few communications, well suited to the activities of drug manufacturers and traffickers and ecologically good
for growing coca. As an area of colonisation, it attracted
workers and their families from other parts of the country on
the look-out for activities that produced more income than the
meagre returns from peasant agriculture in the highlands. Coca
proved an ideal crop. It thrived in the nutrient-poor soils of the
Chapare, where it did not require the sort of elaborate terracing
as in the steep-sided Yungas valleys. Nor did it suffer much
from the pests that tend to bedevil other sorts of agriculture in
tropical or semi-tropical areas. Coca bushes in the Chapare
typically produce three or four harvests a year, and therefore
provide farmers a constant stream of income. Finally, and most
importantly, coca leaves usually command much higher prices
than the legal alternatives: pineapples, bananas, passion fruit,
palm hearts or black pepper.

Coca attracted the sort of inward migration from other parts
of the country that the 1960s colonisation schemes had been
designed to foster. Between 1967 and 1987, the population of
the Chapare expanded nearly tenfold from 24,000 inhabitants
to nearly a quarter of a million, including seasonal workers.
The increase in coca production was a response to the boom in
demand for cocaine, mainly in the United States but also in
Europe, which pushed up prices for the leaf. Although market
prices for coca proved quite volatile over time, even at the low
points they generated more income than the local alternatives,
and much more than subsistence agriculture in the Altiplano.
Coca was also attractive because it grew alongside other sources
of sustenance, so when coca prices were low farmers could
always fall back on other food crops for survival.

The boom in world cocaine demand coincided with the worst economic crisis in living memory in Bolivia. Hyperinflation in the early 1980s plus the impact of the drastic 1985 stabilisation plan brought huge social suffering and widespread unemployment, accentuating the quest for alternative sources of income. A coca farmer of the Chapare in the late 1980s earned an income many times higher than the national average wage. The attractions of migration were obvious, although the relative ease of access of the Chapare to Cochabamba and the Altiplano meant that those who moved to the region did not necessarily do so permanently, maintaining at least a foothold in their communities of origin. Among the migrants who settled the Chapare at this time were large numbers of ex-miners, forced to move from the mining encampments of Potosí and Oruro because of the closure of the mines in the years following 1985. The exact numbers involved are unknown, but a thousand or more miners are thought to have moved to the Chapare at this time. More important than the numbers was the tradition of organisation that the miners brought with them. This was built on the *sindicalista* tradition, and under the leadership of former mineworkers the *sindicalistas* of the Chapare became a formidable force in opposing successive governments' attempts to end coca growing.

The importance of the drugs issue in US domestic politics from the 1980s onwards meant that Bolivia – like Peru and Colombia – came under the strongest pressure from Washington to reduce supplies of coca and cocaine. The system of certification meant that each year the White House had to judge which countries around the world it considered to be 'collaborating' with the United States in the 'war on drugs'. This carried with it the threat that 'non-collaborating' states would no longer receive US economic assistance or support in the funding decisions of multilateral banks like the World Bank. In Bolivia in the early 1980s, preoccupation about drugs took over from that of Communist-inspired subversion as the main issue for the US embassy. The link between drugs production and sectors of the ruling elite in Bolivia had been made manifest by the 1980 military coup, which brought to power a military junta with involvement in the drugs mafia. In 1982, when Ronald Reagan was president, the United States backed a return to democracy in Bolivia in which the Communist Party was a participant in government. In the years that followed, a succession of US ambassadors did their best to force the Bolivian authorities into repressing coca cultivation.

The strategy involved a mixture of interdiction (the cutting of supply lines between Bolivia and Colombia), the forcible eradication of coca, and the offering of inducements for farmers to grow other crops. Highly dependent on US aid flows and other forms of finance from multilateral banks, Bolivian governments judged that they had little option but to heed these strictures. A series of laws were passed outlawing coca cultivation beyond a minimum quantity for traditional domestic consumption. These laws were codified in 1988 by Law 1008, which set a maximum of 12,000 hectares for legal production to meet local demand for coca. Acreages over and above that would be considered illegal. Some would be subject to voluntary eradication programmes with compensation, others to forcible eradication without. US-backed alternative development projects, which involved cultivating tropical fruits, were known as *asociaciones*. The law, however, ruled out the use of herbicide spraying and laid emphasis on the importance of alternative development in areas like the Chapare. The actual involvement of US personnel on the ground in Bolivia has always been a matter of some controversy, but there was little doubt as to who was calling the shots. By the control point just outside Villa Tunari, the billboard advising people to inform on those continuing to grow coca is signed not by the Bolivian authorities but by the US Department of Justice.

The campaign to eradicate coca in the Chapare moved into high gear when Hugo Banzer became president in 1997. He unveiled what he called the Dignity Plan (*Plan Dignidad*), which anticipated a policy of 'zero coca' within five years. The pace of forcible eradication in the Chapare was stepped up as a result, and the region placed under direct military control. The battle lines were thus drawn with the *cocaleros* and the six geographical *federaciones* into which they were organised. The period of greatest confrontation was probably between 1998 and 2000, although clashes continued through at least to 2002 and have taken place intermittently ever since. Local informants tell of how their communities were continuously harassed by the army and drugs police as the slow process of manual eradication pushed ahead. Although eradication never got close to the aim of 'zero coca', it was certainly true that acreages were greatly reduced in the Chapare in the late 1990s. The figures are proudly presented to (a carefully vetted) public at the small museum that has been opened within the army base at Chimore, in the heart of the Chapare. They claim that from 1998 onwards, 25,000 hectares were eradicated. In terms of numbers arrested, cocaine maceration pits and factories destroyed and the volume of coca burned, the military's most successful year was 2001. But the violent nature of the eradication programme led to deaths on both sides.

The eradication campaign helped contribute to the rise to national prominence of Evo Morales and what became the MAS. As the government's campaign of repression against coca intensified from the late 1980s onwards, the *cocaleros* became more organised and militant. They became an important force within the main peasant confederation, the CSUTCB, using this as a platform to oppose eradication. A key argument was the importance of coca to the indigenous identity, a discourse which found wide sympathy in other sectors of the population critical of the way in which successive governments had been forced by the United States to eradicate a crop so important to Bolivia's culture, economy and way of life. Having won control of the CSUTCB in 1992, the coca growers set out to build a political party to represent their interests and to act as an adjunct to their *bloqueos* and other forms of direct action. Encouraged by international receptiveness to *indigenista* discourse, the *cocaleros* led by Morales and others in the CSUTCB set up the *Asamblea de la Soberanía de los Pueblos* (Assembly for the Sovereignty of Peoples; ASP) in 1995. The ASP wrapped up the votes of people living in the Chapare in the 1995 municipal elections and went on to win four seats in parliament in 1997. In 1999, to conform to the strictures of the electoral authorities, Morales' followers changed their party's name to the MAS, a party that had been registered previously but which had become defunct. In 2002, Morales and the MAS came only a narrow second to Sánchez de Lozada and the MNR in the general elections of that year, constituting thereafter the largest opposition bloc in the Congress. Morales was able to capitalise on a widespread feeling of indignation within Bolivia about support for US-backed policies and the need to shake free of Washington's tutelage. His support was only enhanced when, a few days before voting took place, the then US ambassador, Manuel Rocha, threatened that Bolivia would suffer the consequences if its citizens insisted on electing Morales, a 'narco-terrorist', as their president.

Voices: Radio Soberanía

Gerónimo Anturiano runs the radio station Radio Soberanía in Chiripiri, the self-styled 'Sovereign Voice of the Bolivian Cocalero'. The radio station is deep in Evo country, and speaks for the *Federación del Tropico*, one of the six *federaciones* and the one from which Morales first emerged as a forceful figure in the region. It was being enlarged when I visited to accommodate Sovereign TV, a project by the *cocaleros* to set up their own television station. On the walls of the studio, among posters of Bartolina Sisa (the wife of Tupaj Katari, the 18th century *indigenista* rebel) and Che Guevara, was the painted slogan 'for us the coca leaf is the culture of our ancestors and of our survival.' In the 2002 showdown, the radio station had been destroyed by the army. Around the corner, in the now abandoned village coca market, is the defiant inscription (in Quechua) 'Long live coca, death to all Yankees.'

We have faced no end of conflicts. The first thing they do is to go after the dirigentes *(leaders). At the height of the violence, it was like in those films about Vietnam. There were helicopters, the lot. When Tuto* (President Jorge Quiroga) *shut down the Sacaba market, they then came after us and burned down the radio station. One of the conditions for signing a truce was that they came and repaired it for us.*

They have eradicated a lot of coca around here. The cocales *we have left are deep in the jungle, far from any point of access. We continue to live from coca. They have cut down the plants, but they have not cut off our hands. There'll never be zero coca here. People are trying to cultivate citrus fruit, but the prices are too low, and they simply do not compete with coca. At present the price of coca is higher than it has been for a long time. We use the coca we grow to exchange for other goods: potatoes, even medicines.*

The asociaciones *don't try to cross us; they know we're in earnest. At least we have food to eat here; they won't be able to starve us out.*

Federaciones versus asociaciones

By 2004, a relative calm had returned to the Chapare. While road blocks and clashes with the army were still a relatively fresh memory, the frequency of such confrontations was much more sporadic. The worst crisis of the recent past was in 2002, when the interim government of Jorge Quiroga ordered the closure of the Sacaba coca market, just outside Cochabamba, an incident that led to several deaths and a flurry of road blockages in response. The 2002 elections and the new status won by Evo Morales as de facto leader of the opposition made the new government of Gonzalo Sánchez de Lozada more circumspect in its dealings with the *cocaleros*. The appointment of a new US ambassador, David Greenlee, replacing Rocha, also led to the adoption of a rather more sensitive approach to local politics, as Greenlee seemed to recognise the dangers of social protest spiralling out of control. The fall of Sánchez de Lozada in October 2003 underlined the message that political problems in El Alto, rather nearer to the seat of government than the Chapare, were perhaps a more potent source of danger to US interests in Bolivia; continuance with the 'zero coca' policy also ran the risk of creating too many enemies at the same time. The return of relative peace in the Chapare also reflected Evo Morales' backing for the Carlos Mesa administration during its first year in office, a role sharply criticised by some erstwhile supporters in the Chapare and elsewhere.

No-one knows for sure how many hectares of coca there are in the Chapare, but in 2004, as repression eased and prices rose, the number increased substantially. Some talked of 12,000 hectares, as opposed to 6,000 at the beginning of the year. Much of the cocaine produced in Bolivia is now destined for the European market (via Brazil) rather than for the US market (via Colombia or even Peru). That large numbers of people continue to cultivate coca in the Chapare there is no doubt. However, plots tend to be small (3-5 hectares is the norm) and located far from the main roads and often in the shadow of other vegetation to prevent detection by satellites. But the eradication programme has created shortages of supply, and when we visited coca-producing communities we were told that a *carga* (100 lbs) was worth about 80% more than twelve months earlier. If true, the economic incentives were certainly strong for people to continue planting coca, and in so doing to turn their back on the *asociaciones*.

Voices: The *federaciones*

Asencio Picha is an executive member of the *Federación Centrales Unidas*, based in Shinahota. We met him in the brand-new municipal buildings there, which sports a large plaque saying how the European Union helped construct it.

We continue to plant coca, but the amounts are well down on what they used to be. People's incomes have therefore fallen a lot. Most of us are staying put, but there are lots migrating to Spain. There is no market for selling fruit. Ten pineapples sell for 1 boliviano (about 8 pence). We give the pineapples to the pigs. Coca is our identity; it also has lots of vitamins. The government won't help us market coca. USAID conditions all the support they give, and they are trying to divide us up. But everyone plants coca here, even if it's only 40-50 square metres.

Before we had little to do with the municipality, but now we're more closely involved. We're helping to build bridges and schools. It's a good idea. Before the municipal authorities just pocketed the money, but we now keep a close eye on them. We have adopted a system of participatory budgets.

The programme of alternative development orchestrated by USAID has involved considerable amounts of aid to the Chapare, even though in recent times the proportion of Bolivian cocaine being sent to Europe has increased. According to one source, between 1988 and 2002 a total of US$750 million was spent by USAID in the region, making it the largest focus of aid spending in the Americas, at least in per capita terms. USAID concentrated its attention on building alternative livelihoods to coca, as well as building roads. It conditions receipt of any aid flows to a commitment by the beneficiaries not to plant coca and to sever all ties with the coca-producing *federaciones*. In practice, local observers say that many of those who have taken USAID's money continue to grow coca on the side.

Alternative development projects, run by *asociaciones*, vary enormously in size and sophistication. At one end of the spectrum there are factories like Indatrop, a part Swiss-owned venture producing palm hearts (*palmito*) for consumption in Chile. At the other, there are precarious projects like Jipyapa, where a group of women work long hours for little money, making straw hats. However, as one local observer maintains, their function is the same: "to destroy the *federaciones*". A common criticism of most alternative development projects is that politics takes precedence over production, and that production takes precedence over marketing. Consequently, the economic returns are often ridiculously low in comparison to the money that can be derived from growing coca, with its highly efficient systems of marketing. Many in the region were promised prices for alternative products that have simply not materialised. *Palmito* for instance was supposed to sell at 1.4 Bolivianos (about 10 pence) a bundle, but in fact it sells at 60 centavos. According to one Cochabamba-based economist, "alternative development has gone against all the canons of development economics." There are no adequate markets, either within Bolivia or abroad, for such fruit as oranges and pineapple, and in a show of indignation, growers protested in 2002 by dumping all the produce they could not sell in the main square in Chimore. A community leader lost his life as the army opened fire on the demonstrators.

The European Union, which like USAID has spent large amounts in alternative development, appears less wedded to the idea of forcing people to stop growing coca. Instead it has developed programmes to encourage municipal governance in the various towns of the Chapare. In practice, this has meant providing cash for projects closely associated with the MAS, which has a virtual political monopoly in local government in the region. These resources are geared to improving conditions of life in the more urban areas. The EU also has a programme to promote land titling, a more controversial policy since the *federaciones* are bitterly opposed to it. The *federaciones* remain ultimately responsible for the distribution of land within the six sub-regions into which the Chapare is divided. Members of the *federaciones* pay dues (usually fairly small amounts) which gives them access to land, which is then often sub-divided between family members. Individuals in the community are subject to collective decisions at the level of the *federación*, a factor which gives it considerable power over them. These, too, are seen as *usos y costumbres*. Land titling under the provisions of the *Instituto Nacional de Reforma Agraria* (National Institute of Agrarian Reform; INRA) legislation, introduced in 1996 to regulate land ownership (see Chapter Three), has not gone far in the Chapare, precisely because it seems to undermine the political grip of the *federaciones*. As Asencio Picha in Shinahota says "the INRA is not there to respect *usos y costumbres*."

Voices: The alternative developers

Rudiger Gumz, a German who has worked for many years in Bolivia, is joint head of the European Union's Support Programme for the Strategy for Alternative Development in the Chapare. The programme is scheduled to close in 2006.

We see our job here from a technical point of view. But it is difficult to work with the federaciones *in a technical way. With them, the political vision always comes out on top. In working with the municipalities, we are trying to advance participation, and they (the MAS) represent the people in the Chapare. What we are aiming at it is to give greater management autonomy to social actors in the communities there. We're delighted with what we have achieved, because the type of development that is now going on is more participative and sustainable than before. The municipalities are working really well.*

We have never conditioned our assistance to eradication. We all subscribe to the struggle against drugs, but we see the various elements as independent of one another. Land titling is a difficult area, because the federaciones *feel they are being challenged. But would people prefer to have a land title signed by Carlos Mesa than one by Evo Morales?*

Turning to the Yungas

On the steep hillsides near the town of Coroico, in North Yungas province in the department of La Paz, local farmers are constructing the intricate systems of terracing that enable coca to be grown. The landscape is a patchwork of different sorts of crops that combine subsistence with commercial agriculture. But local observers are in no doubt as to what the main trend is. "Coca is winning out all over," says one local producer in Coroico. "You should see what is going on further down in the vicinity of Arapata and Coripata." The main incentive, of course, is the rise in prices for coca. This gives it a premium over all else.

The pattern of repression in the Yungas has not so far been as drastic or methodical as in the Chapare. Law 1008 defined the Yungas as a 'traditional' area of coca production such as for cultural or medicinal purposes, or for people to chew in order to stave off effects of physical fatigue or altitude. This meant that coca cultivation was not illegal. The general thrust of drug policy in the region gave greater weight to development of alternatives to coca and to policies of crop diversification than to eradication as such. Under the auspices of the United Nations, considerable attention was given to introducing new varieties of high quality coffee into the Yungas, a policy complemented by providing for a variety of other commercial opportunities. The government has sought to exercise strict control over the entry into the Yungas of the chemicals required to make cocaine by means of checks on road traffic coming in from La Paz. The hills and valleys of the Yungas in any case have made it much more difficult to implement the same sort of eradication strategies as in the flatlands of the Chapare. The strength of local community organisation also means that any eradication offensive encounters stiff resistance from the *cocaleros* and their allies in the region. Both under Sánchez de Lozada and then under Mesa, *campesinos* managed to force police detachments to turn back. Because of local pressure, the government has found it difficult to install a new barracks to help it control the routes into the Yungas. Like the Chapare, the Yungas has also turned into a MAS stronghold.

The 2003 UN figures on coca cultivation suggest that whereas acreages were falling in Peru and Colombia as a result of eradication strategies in these countries and levels in the Chapare had bottomed out at a historically low level, this was far from being true of the Yungas. There, the UN reckoned, acreages had increased by 18% from 2002 to 16,200 hectares, whereas in the Chapare the number of hectares fell slightly to 7,300. These conclusions broadly concur with other estimates, both international and local. According to the EU, for example, there were 21,000 hectares of coca in the Yungas, of which 11,000 were 'non-traditional' and therefore illegal. Assuming for a moment that high prices for coca persist and that the economic incentives to plant more coca continue, it is likely only to be a matter of time before the US embassy starts adding to the pressure it exerts on Bolivia to step up coca eradication. Indeed the government's own five-year plan for the Yungas, introduced in late 2004, contemplated just such steps.

In such circumstances, the six *federaciones* of *cocaleros* in the Yungas would probably react strongly, perhaps even more so than those of the Chapare, against the implementation of the sort of policies contained in Banzer's Dignity Plan. Since the dividing line between what is 'traditional' coca and what is not has always been a loose and arbitrary one, producers would seek to defend their rights to produce 'traditional' coca, even if the eventual end-use was making cocaine. The strength of community organisation in the largely Aymara Yungas would probably highlight the 'indigenous' nature of such a conflict more than it did in the Chapare, linking up with longstanding ethnic conflicts in the Altiplano. This looked like a quarrel that Carlos Mesa might try to avoid.

3
The Land Question in Santa Cruz

Travelling northwards out of the city of Santa Cruz along the Avenida Cristo el Redentor (otherwise known as the Avenida Banzer), you could quite easily think you were in Texas. Along the main highway there are car dealerships selling the latest in four-by-fours, US-style shopping malls, gleaming new gas stations, a variety of motels and fast-food outlets, stores offering the latest in agricultural machinery and others providing sophisticated equipment for the oil industry. This is a rather different Bolivia from most other parts of the country, a Bolivia that consciously and confidently emulates US-styled modernity; one factory along the main road even boasts a giant replica Statue of Liberty on its roof.

And Santa Cruz *is* different. For decades, the *cruceño* economy has developed much faster than the Bolivian economy as a whole, attracting immigrants from the rest of the country and even from abroad. Its extensive, highly capitalised agriculture stands in striking contrast with the problems of small-scale peasant agriculture in the highlands. The city of Santa Cruz, with its wide tree-lined avenues spreading out in concentric rings (*anillos*) from the central *plaza*, exudes a sense of urban planning and civic pride. Its political and economic elites have cultivated a sense of regional distinctiveness, at times defying the rest of the country. The green and white flag of Santa Cruz is flown just as much, if not more, as the green, red and yellow national *tricolor*.

But for all its modernity and self-confidence, Santa Cruz has its fair share of social problems. Acute poverty is to be found, especially but not just in rural areas. Immigrant communities from other parts of the country and indigenous groups that have fled their ancestral lands are among the poorest. Teenage Ayoreo girls prostitute themselves along the Avenida Brasil, seeking to survive in a hostile city environment. Young boys try to earn their daily crust in the main square polishing shoes. The proximity of great affluence and indigence makes Santa Cruz the most unequal part of Bolivia, a social divide made deeper by ethnic discrimination against indigenous peoples, especially migrants from the highlands. Beyond the confines of the city inequality of income and wealth is even more stark. Agriculturalists with hundreds of thousands of hectares vie with landless peasants for control of the key economic resource: land.

Growth of the cruceño economy

Fifty years ago Santa Cruz was little more than a small town in a remote part of Bolivia; stretching out from the large central square there was a criss-cross of mud roads lined by humble one-story buildings, their verandas giving on to a single first *anillo*. The city's population was just a few thousand, and until 1956 the department of Santa Cruz was physically unconnected with the rest of Bolivia. To the east, beyond the Rio Grande, was a thousand kilometres of sparsely-populated plains with wide horizons stretching out towards the Brazilian frontier; to the south were the grasslands of the Chaco, where oil had been discovered in the 1930s and which had been the scene of horrendous carnage during the three-year Chaco war with Paraguay (1932-35); and to the north were the largely inaccessible tropical jungles of the Beni.

The main natural assets that triggered the rapid development of Santa Cruz within a single generation – today the city has eight *anillos* – have been coca, hydrocarbons (oil and gas) and land. In the years that followed the 1952 revolution successive governments, with the decided backing of the US government and the Washington-based multilateral agencies, sought to promote economic diversification in Bolivia through the development of agribusiness and oil. The decline in the metallic content of Bolivian tin ores, until then the country's main source of foreign exchange, made such diversification important. Changes in the oil and gas legislation in the 1950s encouraged the development of hydrocarbons, primarily through the activities of Gulf Oil, whose Bolivian assets were nationalised in 1969 to create YPFB. Gas exports to Argentina became one of Bolivia's main sources of foreign exchange and a key source of income for local development in Santa Cruz. The development of agriculture – initially cotton, sugar and cattle ranching – had an even greater transformative effect on Santa Cruz, helping to build up a new, affluent and assertive elite that increasingly became a dominant political force in national politics. The growth in drugs trafficking in the 1970s and early 1980s also brought wealth, albeit illicit, to Santa Cruz. The 1971 coup by then- Colonel Hugo Banzer saw Santa Cruz come of age politically. Banzer, a *cruceño*, ousted the left-ward leaning military government of General Juan José Torres, and presided over a right-wing dictatorship under which Santa Cruz prospered. Through the state Agrarian Bank large amounts of capital were transferred to those involved in agribusiness in the *Oriente* (eastern lowlands), primarily in Santa Cruz but also in the department of the Beni further north.

The expansion of agriculture in Santa Cruz attracted large inflows of migrants from other parts of Bolivia. One of the suppositions of policy in the 1950s and 1960s was that the development of Santa Cruz and other lowland areas would help reduce the pressure on land in the Altiplano. The 1953 Land Reform divided up large estates in the Altiplano and in the inter-Andean valleys, giving land to those who worked it previously as bonded labourers (*peones*). But it did not affect the lowlands, where indigenous tribes were viewed officially as little more than savages. In Santa Cruz colonisation schemes were introduced to encourage migration from poor parts of the *sierra* to specially-designated areas like San Julián to the north-east of Santa Cruz or Yapacaní to the north-west. Other migrants came more spontaneously, attracted by temporary employment opportunities such as work on the sugar or cotton harvests. Helped by a variety of outside agencies, there were also programmes to settle migrants from other parts of the world in an area with seemingly limitless land but where labour was in chronically short supply. In the 1950s, groups of Japanese settlers built colonies in the fertile region to the north of Santa Cruz. Mennonites also established themselves, generating a justified reputation as assiduous and skilful farmers. In the 1970s, there were plans – which ended up becoming highly contentious – to settle white farmers from South Africa in Santa Cruz as well as members of the fervently pro-US Hmong mountain tribes displaced from Laos and Vietnam after the Vietnam War.

The constant expansion of the agricultural frontier meant that initially there was no problem of land shortage in Santa Cruz. Activities like cattle rearing gave rise to enormous extensions of privately-owned land, with estates of up to half a million hectares. The development of soya cultivation in Santa Cruz from the 1980s onwards also encouraged huge concentrations of arable land, especially in the plains to the east of Santa Cruz. Soya cultivation, which has become one of Bolivia's top export activities, does not lend itself to small-scale production, and the only small farmers to benefit are those producing seed that is sold to the large-scale producers. The provisions of the 1953 agrarian reform, which expropriated landed estates and limited the scale of private land ownership elsewhere in Bolivia, were never applied in the lowlands.

Regionalism and elite power

The expansion of agriculture in Santa Cruz gave rise to a number of powerful lobbying organisations that skilfully profited from political opportunities to further the interests of their members. One such organisation is the *Federación de Ganaderos de Santa Cruz* (Federation of Livestock Farmers of Santa Cruz; Fegasacruz), which represents the cattle-rearing community. Most agribusiness sectors have such organisations, and these in turn are represented by the powerful *Camara Agropecuaria del Oriente* (The Eastern Chamber of Agriculture; CAO), an umbrella organisation that campaigns for landed interests from the eastern lowlands as a whole. The interests of Santa Cruz are also pursued at a more overtly political level by an influential civic association, the *Comité Pro Santa Cruz*. Organisations like Fegasacruz and the CAO both belong to the *Comité Pro Santa Cruz*, as does the *Camara de Industria y Comercio* (Cainco) which since the capitalisation of YPFB included members from foreign-owned oil and gas companies. All Bolivian departments have their *comités cívicos* to stand up for their regional interests, but the *Comité Pro Santa Cruz* has always been by far the most powerful, reflecting the buoyancy of the department's economy and the assertiveness of its local elite. At certain points in the last 50 years, the *Comité Pro Santa Cruz* has even threatened secession when it has felt the interests of Santa Cruz were not being taken adequately into account by governments in La Paz. Such regional tensions became more acute during left-wing rather than right-wing governments, although in recent years most governments have sought to avoid such confrontations by ensuring that *cruceño* interests are well represented at cabinet level.

Nevertheless, pressure for greater regional autonomy has built up in recent years, especially since the overthrow of Sánchez de Lozada whose MNR party was strong in Santa Cruz. The left in Santa Cruz, by contrast, has always been weak. Traditionally, the COD has been controlled by the *fabriles*, but most industrial employment in Santa Cruz depends one way or another on agroindustry. By contrast, peasants and rural workers have tended to play a fairly marginal role, though this too has been changing in recent years.

Socially and culturally, there have long been attempts to identify the particular nature of what is termed *la cruceñeidad*. Such virtues are extolled on a plaque in the main square on the wall of the September 14 Cultural Club and entitled 'Such is Santa Cruz'. This hails the 'blessed soil' of Santa Cruz, the 'birthplace of famous visionaries' and the spirit of 'honest everyday toil' that 'burns in the blood' of *cruceños*. The Club is one of the main venues for the various business organisations that back up the *Comité Pro Santa Cruz*. One of the more strident organisations both in its message and methods is the *Unión Juvenil Cruceña* (Union of Santa Cruz Youth) which in recent years has helped propagate the notion of the 'Camba nation'. The Cambas were originally the indigenous settlers along the banks of the Piraí river, where modern Santa Cruz is built. Cambas have long been taken to represent the essence of Santa Cruz in contraposition to the 'collas', a term derived from Collasuyo, one of the four divisions of the Inca empire which roughly corresponded to the highlands of present-day Bolivia. This idealised view of the past has often been used to drum up a strong sense of local identity. The contrast between cambas and collas has a poignant and current message in a society where a large proportion of the population, especially the poorest sectors, are indigenous migrants from the highlands.

It is unsurprising that many *cruceños* feel resentment towards political control from La Paz, or that the local elites are good at whipping up demands for greater autonomy. According to figures from the *Instituto Nacional de Estadísticas* (National Statistics Institute; INE), Santa Cruz represented a quarter of the national economy (in terms of output) in 1988. By 1998, this had risen to over 30%, and at the time this writing the proportion must have reached at least a third. The growing economic and demographic weight of Santa Cruz will have important long-term implications, not least for politicians in La Paz who would like to redistribute wealth from Bolivia's wealthier departments to its poorer ones. Debates over the onus of taxation are particularly germane to regionalist pressures. These lay at the heart of regional protests against the Mesa government in 2004 and 2005, whose plans to fill the yawning fiscal deficit through higher taxes on land and hydrocarbons output met with tenacious resistance from the *cruceño* elite.

Conflicts over land

The issue of land and how it is distributed may have been tackled in some parts of Bolivia under the agrarian reform, but the issue is still very much alive and rising up the political agenda in Santa Cruz. The occupation by the local *Movimiento Sin Tierra* (Landless Peasants Movement; MST) of three BP-owned oil compounds in August 2004 gave wide publicity to the issue, but did little to resolve the problem as such. If anything, it served to harden attitudes and to stiffen the resolve of local elites not to submit to this sort of offensive, which they have inevitably termed 'terrorism'.

No longer is the agricultural frontier in Santa Cruz limitlessly expandable, in spite of the relatively low population densities in much of the department. Land conflict here takes different forms but essentially it highlights competing claims against the continued expansion of agribusiness. The boom in soya production since the 1980s has certainly heightened the salience of such conflict, but these claims are also directed against other groups, especially the cattle ranchers, those companies – many from Brazil – extracting timber, those seeking to exploit mining opportunities and those using the land for purely speculative purposes.

Land conflict has been particularly intense in three main

areas, although it is by no means limited to these. The first is to the north-east of Santa Cruz city in the province of Ñuflo de Chávez, an area with a strong presence of indigenous groups (Guarayos) but where there have been important inroads by soya producers, timber extractors as well as groups, including Mennonites, seeking to colonise the land. This is largely forest land, poorly suited to extensive agriculture, where mono-cultivation of soya is leading to severe problems of land degradation. As in other areas of north-eastern Santa Cruz, the soya boom has brought with it the acquisition (usually illegally) of large farms by foreign (usually Brazilian) interests. The second area is to the north and north-west of Santa Cruz, in the provinces of Ichilo and Sara. This is essentially a struggle for land between small-scale peasant producers, many of whom settled this highly productive land 30 or 40 years ago, and large landowners, who were granted extensive holdings during the Banzer dictatorship (1971-78) in return for political support. These frequently lack valid titles to the land they occupy. Some of this land is forestry reserve, like El Choré, but is increasingly being taken over by livestock ranchers. A third area of conflict is to the south of Santa Cruz in the province of Cordillera, where cattle ranchers also vie with indigenous groups (Guaraní) for the control of land. Rural labourers live here in semi-slavery on large farms. According to the journalist Edgar Ramos, this is a case of "total poverty, zero rights".

Conflict over land has become more bitter, and perhaps better publicised, since the initiation of land seizures by the MST over the last ten years. The MST began the policy of occupying unused or under-used land ten years ago in the Gran Chaco region of Tarija, to the south of Santa Cruz. Its leader there was Angel Durán. Although by no means a carbon copy of the better-known Brazilian Movimento Sem Terra, the Bolivian MST used the same name and adopted many of the same sort of practices. In the Gran Chaco, there were large concentrations of land, much of it idle. Although many of those involved in the

MST originally hail from parts of Bolivia other than Santa Cruz (or at least their parents did), they are usually people who have repeatedly sought to settle the land there but either have been unable to achieve legal titles or have been thrown off the land by large landowners. Most work as agricultural labourers. The MST has been particularly active in the area to the north of Santa Cruz, where peasant producers are under strong economic pressure. Partly because they have little or nothing to lose, their politics have become radical. They have resorted to extreme measures, such as occupying foreign-owned oil wells, to dramatise their plight. As in Brazil, there are signs that land occupations are pushing landowners to arm themselves to protect their land or to employ armed vigilantes to do this for them. In such circumstances, it is hardly surprising that MST militants are beginning to arm themselves too. The struggle for land could easily become a very violent business.

Voices: The MST

Wilfor Coque is a member of the MST. In 2000, he was one of those who occupied land in the area of Ichilo, to the north-west of Santa Cruz.

Most of the land in Ichilo is designated as forestry reserves. Many landowners have acquired concessions on forest land, depriving small farmers and the indigenous of access to the land. Some of the land was up for sale on the Internet in 2000, when everyone knew that the land could not legally be sold. Businessmen and livestock ranchers have accumulated large tracts of land, and the INRA has given them legal titles. The law is routinely overturned by those with access to power at the national level. Because land was lying idle, we decided to set up the MST, and to give land to those who have none. I have been involved now for four years. The important thing to say about land occupations is that they happen on land which is being used for speculative purposes. In the medium to longer term, we hope that the government will give titles to those who have occupied land because they had none or their lands were insufficient. And we'll continue occupying the land until this happens. They won't stop us.

Much of the debate about landholding in Santa Cruz revolves around the 1996 INRA law, which modified the original 1953 agrarian reform law in some important respects. Under the 1953 law, it was legal for peasants to occupy land that was not in productive use and then appeal to the land reform authorities to recognise their legal claim to settle that land. In those areas settled in Santa Cruz by small-scale producers from the 1950s onwards (not official colonisation schemes), many settlements grew up on privately-owned land not being used for productive purposes. The 1996 legislation brought some important changes. It sought to develop property holding on the basis of land titling and the elimination of titles acquired fraudulently. This was called *saneamiento* (literally, 'cleansing'). Although the new law included provisions linking ownership to the productive use of land, it fell to the state – not to the peasants seeking to occupy land – to define whether land was being used productively or not. Those like MST members, who were occupying land without seeking prior permission from the INRA, would therefore be acting illegally.

Both settled peasant producers and indigenous groups in Santa Cruz – and elsewhere in the *Oriente* – are usually keen to avail themselves of the INRA to acquire land titles through *saneamiento*. In this respect, their response has differed markedly from the Altiplano where the INRA law has been much criticised by both leaders and rank and file (see Chapter Five). Unlike the Altiplano, lowland smallholders and indigenous tribes have never had access to land titling, and believe that official recognition of their land will provide them with security and enable them to pass on their land to their descendants when they die. According to Roberto Mercado, a smallholder on a plot near El Torno (south-west of Santa Cruz) "the main thing about land titling is the guarantee of having somewhere to live." Roberto, who was born in Tarija, lost his land when he was obliged to spend three years doing military service. *Saneamiento*, which involves defining the exact size of a plot and resolving any conflicting claims, is supposed to be carried out free of charge to those requesting it, but many small farmers seem prepared to pay for it rather than depend on the whims and clientelism of local officials. For indigenous groups, *saneamiento* has the important advantage of affording recognition of their rights to territory (*Territorios Comunitarias de Orígen*, TCOs). The process of *saneamiento* is supposed to be complete by 2006, the tenth anniversary of the INRA Law coming into force. As of late 2004, only a tiny fraction of land in Santa Cruz had been subject to *saneamiento*. Indigenous groups had benefited rather more than small-scale producers in terms of hectares adjudicated. Some peasant farmers said they were afraid that if they did not achieve land titles by 2006 they would face the risk of their land being taken over by the state.

Voices: Small-scale producers

Travelling south-west from Santa Cruz along the old highway to Cochabamba you soon reach El Torno. This is an area of small-scale peasant agriculture. Much of the land had previously been farmed for cotton during the first Banzer government, but by the 1980s it was being settled by peasants from other parts of Bolivia. Today much of the land is given over to growing citrus, especially oranges. The pot-holed road to the community of Alto Villa Barrientos twists and turns among the palm trees and citrus groves. Although the valley looks green enough, the community suffers from chronic lack of water. We met the community leaders at their meeting hall, a brick building with a corrugated iron roof and a mud floor. Don Pablo, one of the elder members and community president, did most of the talking.

For us saneamiento *is one of our top goals. We want to apply the Ley INRA as soon as possible. The timeframe runs out in 2006, and we are very worried what will happen to us if we do not get land titles by then. We are prepared to pay people to do the* saneamiento *rather than go through the local authorities. The people who run INRA are in league with the local political parties and we don't trust them.*

*The situation has improved a bit under Carlos Mesa, but the whole thing (*saneamiento*) is running way behind schedule. By now they should have completed 70%, but they've scarcely done 40%. The authorities give priority to giving titles to those with the most money to pay them. It's a business.*

Here we stand by the sindicato. *For us its our natural unit of organisation, ever since 1952. All the families here are members, and we think it is the most democratic way of arranging our affairs. We always go to meetings of the subcentral (in El Torno) and usually to those of the departmental federation in Santa Cruz. With* Participación Popular, *we saw the municipality grow in importance. It was quite divisive, and the aim was to get rid of the* sindicato. *But with* saneamiento, *it's the* sindicato *that matters most.*

Peasant organisations in Santa Cruz are rather more critical of the INRA than indigenous groups, partly because *saneamiento* has tended to favour the latter over the former. They attack the INRA as lacking any autonomy, and say that its decisions over land demarcation are strongly influenced by local elite groups. "If the law was applied as it stands, as the regulations say, there would be more than enough to redistribute to all those who lack land," says Mariano Viana, a small farmer from Velasco province. "The problem is the structure of power which is concentrated in very few hands." Naturally, those working in the INRA reject such accusations, but admit that the organisation is hamstrung by a lack of resources to carry out its mission.

There is little doubt that many landowners act in flagrant disregard for legal norms in a context where there is no effective mechanism for ensuring compliance with the law, still less for appealing against administrative decisions. Restrictions on the amount of land that can be legally held by a single owner are routinely circumvented by the fictitious subdivision of land. Cattle farmers use the practice known as 'cattle tourism' – daily moving the same herd from one property to another – to convince government inspectors that the land is being fully used. The problem of under-use of land is compounded by the acquisition of land for purely speculative purposes, since rising land values have brought their owners substantial gains and landed property can be used as collateral for borrowing for houses and consumer luxuries. At the same time, there have been numerous denunciations of landowners deliberately dodging their tax obligations by subdividing their land into plots that barely come within the official definition of small-scale agriculture.

Indigenous movements in eastern Bolivia have gained importance as political actors since the 1980s, showing themselves capable of standing up for their own particular demands. Such demands are multiple, but they focus on winning recognition of territorial rights, not just to the land surface but to sub-soil rights. In 1982, the Guaraní, Ayoreo, Chiquitano and Guarayo indigenous groups formed the *Confederación Indígena del Oriente Boliviano* (Indigenous Confederation of the Bolivian East; CIDOB), and by the early 1990s the organisation had expanded to include other ethnic groups elsewhere in the lowlands. These forged a place for themselves on the national political map following a 500 kilometre march to La Paz in 1990 from Trinidad, the capital of the Beni. For the indigenous peoples, who received a rapturous reception when they reached La Paz, this was the first time they discovered they had a political voice. "The march did more than anything else to prove to indigenous peoples that they could achieve things," says Mauricio Bacardit, a Catholic priest, "this is where the TCO began." In 1992, a specifically *cruceño* organisation was established, the *Coordinadora Etnica de Santa Cruz* (Committee of Ethnic Peoples of Santa Cruz; CESC), which subsequently added 'popular' to its title to become the CPESC. CPESC has become an important voice of the indigenous movement, in conjunction with CIDOB, and a conduit for a certain amount of financial assistance from the international community.

A more recent development has been the establishment of an umbrella organisation that brings together the various different elements of the rural coalition – peasants, *colonizadores* from the highlands, indigenous groups and the MST – in Santa Cruz and elsewhere in the lowlands, the *Bloque Oriente Boliviano*. As well as having a more diverse group of supporters, the aims of the Bloque are also broader. It stands as a counterpoint to organisations like the CAO. As well as issues of land distribution, it seeks to highlight other matters related to the use of natural resources, including the preservation of forests, the protection of biodiversity, respect for the intellectual property of indigenous groupings and for the full participation of those living on the land in any discussions over the use of sub-soil resources, especially hydrocarbons. A key promotor of the Bloque has been the CPESC, which has a more organised presence than the MST or other peasant organisations. Partly for this reason, the agenda of the Bloque highlights many of the issues of most concern to indigenous groups.

Voices: Indigenous groups

The headquarters of the *Coordinadora de los Pueblos Etnicos de Santa Cruz* (CPESC) is in a run-down part of Santa Cruz close to where the old railway leaves the urban area in the direction of distant Brazil. It is located beyond the fifth *anillo* in a street where barefoot children play in the mud and where horse-drawn carts jostle for space with microbuses. Carlos Cuosacc, one of the leaders of CPESC, is a member of the Chiquitano ethnic group, one of the largest in the organisation which represents indigenous peoples from all over Santa Cruz.

The main goal of CPESC is to achieve national recognition and respect for our territory and the use of natural resources. There is no judicial security in our territories, no norms to provide legal title to our lands.

The 1990 march [from Trinidad to La Paz] was a major development. We were in La Paz for two months. We went there claiming respect. However, we did not get the protective legislation we were demanding. For us, the Ley INRA was a victory. Lots of people lost their lives in the struggle for the law. However it has not resolved our problems. The issue is not just the passage of legislation, but how to get it enforced. There has been no political will to enforce it. The authorities are under the thumbs of the business community. We want protection for our natural resources, not just wood but minerals and hydrocarbons too.

Our main problem in the Chiquitanía is with the cattle farmers and those who exploit wood illegally. With the weight of organisations like Fegasacruz, it's difficult to get a proper hearing. Decisions always tend to favour the latifundistas, *the people with the power. We don't have such conflicts with the* colonizadores *or the* sin tierras. *With them, we have our own ways of resolving disputes when they arise.*

The law says that saneamiento *should be free and that indigenous populations should get priority. But they demand that we have recognised legal status (*personaría jurídica)*, birth certificates and lots of other documents. You can easily spend a week here just to get an identity document. That costs time and money. It's eight hours from our community to Santa Cruz and eight hours back.*

Political time bomb?

The dynamics of the situation suggest the land issue can only get worse. The numbers of those entering Santa Cruz each year in search of work are reckoned by the local press to be 120,000 a year. Even allowing for some exaggeration and assuming that the real figure may even be half that, there is little available land on which these people can settle and make a living for themselves. At the same time, the consequence of mono-cultivation of crops like soya is the depletion of land resources, especially when many farmers simply plant new land when already cultivated land shows signs of nutrient exhaustion. There are already serious signs of land erosion in Santa Cruz. In such circumstances, problems of landlessness are likely to increase, whilst competition for land among existing users – especially the most fertile land – will rise.

Unless the authorities in charge of land distribution are able to take preventative action through some sort of scheme of land redistribution, conflict over land will become increasingly bitter and probably ever more violent. However, there are few signs that land redistribution will happen. The INRA lacks the political clout – and perhaps the political will – to push ahead with the hugely ambitious task of defining property titles over a huge area and resolving disputed claims. Even if agrarian reform was brought to Santa Cruz, it is hard to see how it would ever be carried out.

4
Pensions, *Rentistas* and the Problems of Old Age

In the pitch darkness tiny lights flickered, then gradually grew larger. The night shift at Siglo XX finally emerged from the depths of the mine bleary-eyed into the glare of bright morning sunlight. The miners heaved the ore and rock they had gathered in canvas bags on their backs. Siglo XX (20th Century), for a long time Bolivia's most productive tin mine, was among the many mines closed by the government when tin prices fell in 1985. Yet today there are more people working its ever-diminishing veins than when Comibol shut it down 20 years ago. Nominally *cooperativistas* (cooperative workers), these people in fact work for themselves, seeking to extract enough ore from the inner depths to feed themselves and their families. As we greeted the men, exhausted from their night's work, they seemed in surprisingly good spirits; at least the rise in world tin prices in 2004 had meant that for all the hard work and physical danger involved, they were making slightly more than they had in previous years.

Once the jewel in the crown of tin baron Simón Patiño's empire, today Siglo XX is a rusting monument to a bygone age. Working conditions at Siglo XX are closer to the 16th century than those of the 20th century, let alone the 21st. Within the mine, no proper maintenance is carried out, and rockfalls and injuries are common. The rolling stock that used to carry the workers the 3 kilometres to the mine face and then shift the ore out no longer works, and the air compressors that used to ventilate the mine have long since broken down. Outside, amid the rusting machinery and the derelict sheds, the *cooperativistas* and their families use the most primitive techniques to separate tin ore from rock prior to selling it on, generally at knock-down rates to intermediaries who in turn sell it on to dealers in Oruro. But the rise in tin prices has brought people back to Siglo XX and the neighbouring township of Llallagua from other parts of the country. Despite the danger and the scanty returns, the old mine retains its allure.

The refinery at nearby Catavi stands empty except for a section that now functions as a cooperative, processing ore from the slag heaps of previously extracted rock which still has some mineral content. The former homes of mineworkers stand in ruins, the company store (*pulpería*) is boarded up, the once-proud Teatro Simón Patiño is now used as storage for paperwork. The hospital has been turned over for use by the National University of Siglo XX. Set up at the behest of the FSTMB at the time of the mine closure, it forms part of the national system of higher education. Its student numbers now provide the main source of income in what would otherwise be a ghost town. When Siglo XX closed, the population of Llallagua fell from over 70,000 to just 30,000 as miners and their families left to look for work in other parts of Bolivia.

First to accept redundancy after 1985 and to leave Siglo XX were the youngest miners. The older ones tried to cling on to their jobs in Comibol as best they could, fearful that they would lose their pension entitlements. The death blow came in 1993, when the government came up with sufficient cash to persuade them to accept redundancy terms. They took the money, leaving what was left of the mine to the *cooperativistas*. The closure of Siglo XX and most of the other mines that came under Comibol, with a loss of over 25,000 jobs, spelled the end of a proud union tradition that had played a pivotal role in the country's turbulent politics since the establishment of the FSTMB back in the 1940s. The local union headquarters still stands in the square in Siglo XX, marked by a statue of a miner holding his drill in one hand and a rifle in the other. It too is empty, except for an office used by the *Asociación de Rentistas Mineros de Llallagua*, the former miner pensioners' association, a well-organised grouping that seeks to defend the rights and interests of the older people left behind after closure. Along with pensioners in other mining towns, the *rentistas* have become an active pressure group in defending the interests of those who can no longer work. In a sense, they carry on the tradition of active trade unionism by trying to establish and defend workers' rights.

At a national level, ex-miners provide the backbone of the *Confederación de Rentistas* (Pensioners' Confederation), based in La Paz, which seeks to defend pension entitlements and the interests of old people more generally. They were also the driving force behind a series of high-profile marches by pensioners between 2000 and 2003 to set a minimum national pension of 1,000 Bolivianos. The marches did much to dramatise the economic problems facing the older generation, whose interests are all too often forgotten.

Voices: Retired mineworkers

Prudencio Guzmán, who is 70, belongs to the *Asociación de Rentistas Mineros de Llallagua*. I talked to him and other leaders of the Asociación in the dark room they use as an office in the old building of the FSTMB. Behind his desk was an immaculately embroidered ceremonial Bolivian *tricolor* with the Asociación's name, the date it was established and the official number of its legal recognition.

We have fought for ten years to achieve a basic pension of 1,000 Bolivianos for all workers, and we have not got there yet. We settled for 850 Bolivianos after the march to La Paz. Although as miners we have been on several such marches in the past, it was the first time ever that pensioners have taken to the road. The level of public sympathy for our cause was tremendous.

The Bonosol is certainly a help, but most of the money goes to helping our families. The economic situation here in Llallagua is bleak. We don't spend it on ourselves. We also have free medical assistance, but the problem is that there is no money in the (health) system. All they do is to give you a few pills. There's a big difference between what the law says and what it actually provides.

Problems of old age

Like most places in Latin America, Bolivia is a young country in the sense that a much higher proportion of its population is under the age of 18 than in more developed countries. Only 7% of the population in 2001 was over the age of 60. Bolivia also has a lower life expectancy than many other countries in the region because of its high levels of poverty and the lack of adequate health facilities. For men, the average life expectancy was 61 in 2001, and for women 64. However, there are big variations here; in the rural Altiplano a 45 year-old is probably considered 'old' whereas this is not the case in the main cities. Again, as in most other countries, the age profile of the Bolivian population is changing. Life expectancy is extending, and will probably reach around 80 for men and 85 for women by 2045. By this time the proportion of the population over 60 will be significantly higher than at the moment. One of the factors behind this greater longevity is the pace of urbanisation.

There is no direct correlation in Bolivia between those who are pensioners and those who are old. Pensioners are not necessarily old: people often receive occupational pensions well before they are 60, let alone 65. And old people are not necessarily pensioners: only just over 20% of the elderly are in receipt of a pension, according to figures from HelpAge International. Most old people in Bolivia have neither work nor a pension, and they are among the poorest of the poor. According to official figures, 63% of old people live in poverty, though HelpAge believes that this is a gross understatement. The 2001 census figures give a reasonable numerical profile of the elderly, showing that half of those who are over 60 years old live in rural areas, more than the national average, and a further 25% are involved in domestic activities of one sort or another. But the figures tell us little of the quality of life. A survey undertaken by INE indicates that the old are usually among the poorest members of a community. It also suggests that local authorities give little priority to the needs and interests of elderly citizens.

There is also a gender dimension to the problem of old age. More elderly women than men tend to be poor, because they live longer and have less ability to generate income into old age. Also, women are much less likely than men to be in receipt of an occupational pension. In rural areas they usually have less voice within the community and are more likely to be illiterate. According to Valeria Mealla at HelpAge, "there's a circularity between well-being and participation. You need to have a minimal level of well-being to be able to participate, but you need to participate to access well-being." Older women, she says, are often marginalised.

Voices: A parliament of the old

Don Felipe Bozo, a sprightly 75 year-old, is president of the national 'parliament' for the elderly in Bolivia. Formerly a miner from Huanuni in Oruro, he has also been general secretary of the pensioners' confederation.

We decided to establish the Parliament in May 2001 as a response to the problems facing older people generally. It seeks to establish rights for the elderly. People here value youth, and the older generations just get forgotten. Here we fight for the rights of all old people, not just the rentistas. *We have nine different organisations in each department that belong to the Parliament, which in turn seeks to represent their demands at the level of government. We are also working with other groups of the elderly from other countries. There are nine countries that belong to a Latin American Old People's Network* (Red Latino-americana y del Caribe de Líderes Adultos Mayores) *and we are in constant contact with each other.*

The support of the state for old people is fairly weak. We have written a policy document that we hope will become the basis of a new law. We are working on Congress to get it onto the statute book, but it will require detailed regulation to make it effective. We're also working closely with ECLAC (the United Nations Economic Commission for Latin America and the Caribbean) in Chile on all of this.

Rights for older people

Partly as a result of the activities of people like the *rentistas* and those of NGOs, old people have won certain rights in Bolivia over the years. Often, however, there is a lack of knowledge of what these rights consist of, an absence of relevant documentation by which to claim them, and an unwillingness to recognise such rights on the part of those who should heed them. In theory, elderly people are able to claim a series of discounts, both for basic services (such as water and electricity) as well as transport. In practice, few benefit from these; private providers are unwilling to pay for such concessions and people lack the means to insist that their rights are respected. Old people should also receive help with their housing costs, but this applies to owners only, not tenants. Again, old people are supposed to receive special healthcare treatment free of charge, but the health system is so bereft of resources that such treatment amounts to little, even if help and advice are available.

An important innovation for the elderly in Bolivia has been the Bonosol, an annual payment made to those of 65 years or older financed by the proceeds of the capitalisation of former state companies (see Chapter One). The Bonosol is paid to all

Bolivians as a right of citizenship, and is not subject to a means test. When the Bonosol was first introduced in 1996 at the end of the first Sánchez de Lozada administration, many sceptics dismissed it as just an electoral bribe by a government desperate to win re-election. Since then, however, it is a scheme – unique in Latin America – that many have come to value. When Sánchez de Lozada stepped aside and the subsequent Banzer administration sought to change the system, there was a strong outcry of protest. At the time of writing, the Bonosol was worth 1,800 Bolivianos (around US$227) for every old person, which would mean an annual income supplement of nearly US$460 for an elderly couple. Particularly in terms of rural purchasing power, this is a substantial amount of money, and a welcome supplement to families looking after elderly parents.

Apart from the rather obvious point that most Bolivians never reach the age of 65, one of the main drawbacks of the Bonosol scheme is that many of the older generation lack the basic documentation to claim it. Claimants have to prove their age by submitting a birth certificate, but many older people – especially those living in remote rural areas – lack such official documents. Indeed, birth certificates were only introduced in 1943, before which the only proof of age was a certificate of baptism. The introduction of the Bonosol has, it must be said, pushed the authorities to take active steps to remedy this problem by providing old people with the necessary documentation. Most old people do not spend the Bonosol themselves, rather they share it with their younger relatives.

Privatising pensions

Whilst introducing the Bonosol, the first Sánchez de Lozada government also set about the privatisation of pensions, following the model pioneered by Chile in the 1980s. This was but one element of the economic liberalisation package promoted in most Latin American countries by the World Bank. Consequently, at the end of 1996, the government introduced a new pensions law which shifted the responsibility for administering and paying pensions to the private sector. In future, workers would be obliged to open up private pension plans with foreign-run pension fund administrators (AFPs), which would also be responsible for administering the collectively-owned Bonosol funds. Previously, workers had received pensions paid directly from the Treasury. These were topped up by payments from corporately-run complementary funds (*cajas*) which also provided healthcare in some professions and industries. The *cajas*, whose administration had not always been that transparent, faced serious problems of liquidity at the time. This was also true of the basic state pension fund. According to the architects of the new system, the old pension regime was financially unviable, given the falling ratio of people in formal employment to those with a right to claim pensions and other social benefits. They also argued that a system of private pensions would help foster a local capital market by generating local funds for investment.

The immediate effect of the pensions reform, however, was to add to the public sector deficit, a problem that also arose with pension privatisation in other countries. While all new contributions into the pensions system went into the AFPs as anticipated by the law, the state remained responsible for the payment of existing pension obligations to old people. The fiscal difficulties that Bolivia faced in the years after 1996 – in 2003 the deficit was close to 9% of GDP – were in large measure attributable to the Sánchez de Lozada pension reform. Only in the longer term would the AFPs be called upon to assume full responsibility for all pension payments.

The new system also altered criteria of eligibility for pensions. It established 65 as the pensionable age, whereas previously a pension was payable once a worker had fulfilled a statutory number of contributions into the pension fund. In the case of miners, for instance, it had been possible to retire at the age of 50 or even earlier, assuming that an employee had made at least 180 contributions into the pension fund. The final pension received depends on the number of years worked and the final salary earned. For people reaching senior positions a pension provided a reasonable income in old age. But according to Víctor López, the former executive secretary of the FSTMB and himself a 77 year-old pensioner, most ex-miners could expect a retirement pension of around 300 Bolivianos (US$45) a month, and then have to fight for it to be paid promptly.

The way the new system was designed created a large group of people who were at the time below retirement age. Known as the 'sandwich generation', they fell between two stools. They were workers whose retirement date came after the introduction of the new system and who had not paid the requisite number of contributions under the old system to qualify for a pension. However, they enjoyed no pension rights under the new system since they could not afford to make the necessary contributions to the AFPs. There are some 25,000 workers in this category. Their plight was dramatised in March 2004 when one of their number, Eustaquio Picachuri, an ex-miner, strapped dynamite to his body and blew himself up in the Congress building, killing himself and others standing nearby. This was one of the first ever known cases of a suicide bombing in Latin America. Picachuri had been demanding that he be repaid the contributions he had made into the old pension system which had been rendered effectively worthless. His death stung the government of Carlos Mesa into issuing a decree promising to provide compensation to members of the sandwich generation.

Of course, those who receive some sort of occupational pension are only a small minority of those who reach old age. In a sense, they are the lucky ones, even though the pensions they receive are fairly inadequate in enabling them and their families to meet their daily needs. Those who work in the informal sector of the economy and therefore make no pension contributions, receive no payments. Even in urban areas where there is more formal sector employment, the vast majority of workers find themselves in the informal sector and enjoy little or no provision for old age or access to the welfare facilities managed by the *cajas*. Indeed, one of the main features of the job market since the liberalisation of the economy began in 1985 has been the expansion of the informal sector at the expense of the formal. Even in the formal sector, some employees choose to opt out of the contributory system because they cannot afford the monthly payments.

On the road

The campaign to establish a minimum living pension, adjustable to the loss of purchasing power through inflation, first began in 1992, but only gained real momentum after 2000. At that time, the basic pension payable was 350 Bolivianos a month, with amounts varying between 120 and 280 Bolivianos for surviving widows of former pensioners. Then, 350 Bolivianos was the equivalent of around US$60 a month. Former mineworkers, alongside former factory workers and others, set a target of establishing a basic pension of 1,000 Bolivianos with a system of annual increments that would rise in inverse proportion to the amount of the basic pension. In other words, those with the lowest pensions would receive proportionately more, and those receiving high pensions would get less. When this idea failed to elicit a positive response from the Banzer government, those involved in the campaign decided to organise a pensioners' march from Oruro to La Paz, 235 kilometres across the desolate Altiplano.

As it happened, the so-called 'march for survival' took place in three separate phases. In each case, the march was resumed when the government failed to honour promises it had made to call the previous one off. The first march took place in August 2000. It was suspended when the marchers reached the town of Caracollo, 37 kilometres from Oruro. Stung by the bad publicity of elderly people with blisters marching in the rain, the government sent a high-level team of ministers and officials to negotiate. An agreement was reached whereby the basic pension would be increased to 550 Bolivianos per month and the idea of the inversely proportional increments was accepted. But the government later backtracked on this, paying the increased pension only to ex-miners. In March 2001, the marchers resumed their protest, this time starting out at Caracollo. With 3,000 pensioners on the road, it covered the next 91 kilometres to the town of Patacamaya over several days. Another government delegation was dispatched amid the glare of media attention. At Patacamaya a new deal was agreed whereby all pensioners would receive a minimum payment of 850 Bolivianos, made retroactive to the date of the previous march.

The march was once again resumed in January 2003, following steps by the government to change the system of indexation of pensions to reduce costs to the Treasury by getting rid of its link to the dollar. This time, the marchers reached the town of Calamarca, 46 kilometres further on. On the night of January 5, police and troops intervened to stop the march by forcibly bussing the protestors back to Oruro. The manoeuvre failed, but in the process two buses crashed killing six pensioners and four others. On January 17, the marchers, then numbering some 20,000, reached El Alto and La Paz.

Amid a blaze of bad publicity and facing a tricky national public order situation, the Sánchez de Lozada government finally agreed to the marchers' demands. It resorted to the earlier system of indexation, agreeing to indemnity payments to the families of those who had died during the course of the march. In the end, the marchers settled for the 850 Bolivianos, leaving their target of 1,000 Bolivianos for the future.

Voices: Women pensioners

Antonia Ramos Mollo is 80 years old and a grandmother. She took part in the march of the *rentistas*. Her family tried to dissuade her from taking part, but she insisted. She recounts how the authorities tried to detain the march in Calamarca.

They tried to stop us there, but we were sleeping away from the main group so they never came after us. The next day we left for La Paz, furious about what had happened the previous night. We had no food, but people offered us food as we went along. That night we stayed in a village school. People played music and sang songs to keep our spirits up. But the distances between places were long, and it was extremely hard going because it rained a lot.

When we got to La Paz, the reception was quite extraordinary. We slept in the university. It was a great victory, and I would do it again if I am still here to do so. Most of us on the march were women. The men do not have the same spirit as us.

Swimming against the tide?

Bolivia provides impressive examples of activism among older people, but also raises serious questions about how to translate the language of rights into improved living standards for the elderly, and how to finance the welfare of a social group that is not only needy but increasingly numerous.

Apart from certain groups of pensioners – notably ex-miners – old people are notoriously difficult to organise. They lack a sense of collective identity and purpose, and have few reasons for coming together physically. Events like the Oruro to La Paz marches are not the norm. "The important thing is to ensure that they have a voice in the community," says Valeria Mealla. "But that depends on their own feelings of status and self-esteem." For Víctor López, the most important thing is for pensioners to act together: "if it's not a united struggle, we'll just get picked off (…) we have to resist the temptation for each group just to protect its own little patch."

As Bolivia shifts rapidly in the direction of becoming an urban country, the standing of old people in society is likely to come increasingly into doubt. "This is why things like the Bonosol are important," says Mealla. "Old people have gained rights, even though most are unaware of the fact." Rights like free medical help for the elderly (*Seguro Médico Gratuito de Vejez*) exist in theory, but as a report by the Ombudsman's Office makes plain, most people do not manage to take full advantage of them and where free help is provided by hospitals it is often not reimbursed by the government. The draft legislation that Don Felipe Bozo and others have been working on would represent an important step towards affirming rights (especially in the field of abuse of elderly people), but the real challenge is in the areas of implementation and enforcement.

The funding of welfare provision for the elderly also raises major difficulties. As the state comes under constant pressure from bodies like the IMF to rein in government spending, there is pressure to cut rather than expand public services to the old, and for the foreseeable future pensions payments will continue to be a major drain on public finances. Privatised pensions, meanwhile, will cater only for a very small proportion of the population. Even the future of the Bonosol may be in doubt as the numbers reaching old age continue to increase. According to forecasts by INE, the number of people reaching 65 by the year 2050 will be five times that of 2000, whilst the total population will have doubled. Unless the profitability of former state companies rises in line with the increase in the numbers of those eligible to receive the Bonosol (an unlikely scenario), the value of payments is set to decline. Little thought appears to have been given to the future of the scheme over the next 15 years, let alone between now and 2050.

5

Aymara 'Nationalism' and Land in the Altiplano

Just outside the Altiplano town of Achacachi, a now rather weather-worn graffiti proclaims Gonzalo Sánchez de Lozada to have been 'the new Melgarejo'. Mariano Melgarejo was a mid-19th century dictator who sought to 'privatise' community lands on the Altiplano and use them to reward his followers. In seeking to institute private property Melgarejo, it should be said, was following the example of liberal land reformers in other countries in Latin America, and the policy of dividing up indigenous communities and promoting private land ownership did not stop when Melgarejo was hounded from office by thousands of angry peasants in 1871. Still, for some at least in Achacachi, there were parallels to be drawn with more recent times.

In the period after 2000, Achacachi, a busy commericial centre close to the shores of Lake Titicaca and capital of Omasuyos province, became indelibly associated in the minds of many with the resurgence of Aymara nationalism and the figure of Felipe Quispe. Otherwise known by his assumed title 'El Mallku' (this means 'the condor' or leader in Aymara), Quispe rose to prominence as a forceful peasant leader in the late 1990s. Through demonstrations, road blocks and other methods of protest, Quispe sought to assert the autonomy of the Aymara 'nation', harking back in his public utterances to the struggles of his people against the k'aras, the Aymara word for 'whites'. Reflecting the resurgence of indigenous movements elsewhere in Latin America, and indeed elsewhere in Bolivia,

Quispe has helped push the issues of ethnic identity and land rights to the top of the country's political agenda. As we shall see, the quest to re-found Collasuyo is grounded in the realties of contemporary Bolivian politics.

Land problems and policy in the Altiplano

The 1953 Land Reform sought to abolish peasant servitude, to eliminate large private estates and to distribute land to those who lacked it. However, its effects varied around the country. As we saw in Chapter Three, in the eastern lowlands it led to migrant peasants and indigenous groups living cheek by jowl with large-scale commercial farmers producing (largely) for export. In the western highlands, the agrarian reform made peasant producers owners of their land by abolishing feudal labour relations on the estates (*haciendas*), where *sindicatos* became the main form of social organisation. The agrarian reform, however, did not affect the traditional communities with their *ayllus,* many of which also adopted the *sindicato*. The reform led to a system of small-scale agriculture (*minifundismo*) of families living in local communities. This is the most typical form of land ownership in the Altiplano today, although plot sizes vary substantially according to the type of agriculture practiced. Around Achacachi and along the shores of Lake Titicaca, where communities produce crops both for subsistence and the market, plots are typically very small. In many places *minifundios* have been successively subdivided between one generation and another, and people even refer to *surcofundios*, a *surco* being a single row of crops. In other parts of the Altiplano, especially further to the south towards Oruro and the north of Potosí, where livestock rearing (mainly llamas and alpacas) is the norm, units of landholding are larger.

In most parts of the Altiplano, problems of access to land and water are chronic. There is strong demographic pressure on available land, particularly good pasture that can be irrigated. This has led to an over-exploitation of good land, which has the effect of depleting its fertility over time. There is a serious problem of land degradation and the attendant one of salinisation. This matters less in areas of livestock rearing, but is critical in reducing the productivity of crop farming. New patterns of agriculture that respond primarily to urban demand can make things even worse. For example, dairy farming involves the cultivation of fodder for cows, which in turn reduces the land available for subsistence agriculture and leads to more intensive use of the little good land that remains. Climatic change on the Altiplano as well as the effects of free-market reforms in agriculture have also hit peasant farmers.

In fact, the overall population on the Altiplano has remained fairly stable over recent years. This is because of the numbers who have left their communities and family farms in the search for employment and a better life elsewhere. Traditionally, the Yungas provided a demographic safety valve, allowing families to settle in these subtropical valleys and to diversify into other types of agriculture, especially coca. The city of La Paz, less than 100 kilometres from Achacachi and other communities near Lake Titicaca, also provided an important refuge for surplus population. The rapid growth of El Alto in particular has absorbed large numbers of migrants from surrounding rural areas. But *comuneros* (community members) from the Altiplano have moved much further afield in the search for income. Some moved to the Chapare to produce coca in the 1970s and 1980s, others migrated to Santa Cruz. Buenos Aires and other Argentine cities are also home to hundreds of thousands of Bolivians, many from the highlands, where they are frequently victim to racial prejudice and exploitation.

A variety of policy packages have been adopted over the years to try to resolve some of the problems of Altiplano agriculture, usually focusing on improving production and marketing. Although there have been some successes and commercial activities have increased, most Altiplano farmers and their families remain among the poorest people in the country. Often it is the younger and better educated who migrate to the cities and other parts of Bolivia, leaving their parents behind. One of the more recent government initiatives was the 1996 INRA Law. Enacted at the tail end of the first Sánchez de Lozada government, this began as part of a dialogue between peasant organisations and the state over how to reformulate the original 1953 land reform legislation, which was widely regarded as bureaucratic and ineffective. But as time passed, new policies were placed into the INRA basket, particularly in response to pressures from land-owning lobbyists and organisations like the World Bank. Issues like land titling and property rights gained prominence. Several of the more participatory ideas, such as having input from peasant unions, were dropped.

Peasant organisations from the Altiplano and elsewhere saw the new law as a threat, and no sooner had it been promulgated than they started campaigning for it to be rescinded. This hostility contrasted with the broad acceptance with which the new law was greeted in the lowlands. The TCO responded to the need to protect un-demarcated indigenous lands, but in the highlands most indigenous-based communities already possessed land titles. Apart from one or two more remote places in the Altiplano where communal land ownership still prevailed, there were no attempts to create TCOs. Peasant communities in the Altiplano saw the INRA Law as yet another attempt, in the tradition of Melgarejo, to undermine their traditional structures, their *usos y costumbres*.

The first Sánchez de Lozada government passed two other laws that had a direct impact on the Altiplano. The first of these was the Law of Popular Participation. Popular Participation involved heightening the role played by municipalities in rural affairs, greatly expanding the number of rural municipalities and making more money available for local, especially rural, development. Until 1994, when the new law came into effect, local mayors and town councils were largely decorative, lacking the resources needed to take on a significant role at the local level. As well as redirecting the flow of resources from the state, Popular Participation also became the channel through which debt relief funds could be used for poverty relief under the Highly Indebted Poor Country (HIPC) scheme. In spite of petty corruption at the local level, most communities have used Popular Participation to push ahead with local development projects.

The system is designed to include grass-roots organisations – including *sindicatos* and *ayllus* – in decision-making at the local level. These are known as *Organizaciones Territoriales de Base* (OTBs). Nevertheless, in some places, the *ayllu* has emerged as a focus for hostility to the new local structure, especially where the jurisdictions of municipalities and *ayllus* do not coincide. It can also lead to frictions between mayors and OTBs, not least on the uses to which money should be put. In the town of Guaqui, for instance, the oversight committee decided to throw out the mayor because he was of no use. However, the mayor refused to resign. It was only under the greatest pressure that he was prevailed upon to go. While such conflicts are not uncommon, in many other places mayors and OTBs have managed to see eye to eye.

Voices: The local mayor

Leandro Chacalluca is the mayor of Ancoraimes. Situated just to the north of Achacachi on the edge of Lake Titicaca, Ancoraimes is the second largest town in the province of Omasuyos. Chacalluca was elected as candidate for the *Union Cívica Solidaridad* (Civic Solidarity Union; UCS), but then disavowed his previous party links. The district has 15,000 inhabitants in 58 communities. It straddles the eastern *cordillera* of the Andes, and includes communities in the higher Yungas as well as along the shoreline of Lake Titicaca. Ancoraimes is generally reckoned to be among Bolivia's best performing municipal governments.

When I was elected in 1999, there were lots of problems of governability and corruption. There was a need to break with this tradition. There was also a lot of inequality between communities. We have managed to reduce this. Most communities now have drinking water, electricity and access roads. The Municipal Law was imposed from above. These are formalities. What we need to do is adapt the law to our own practices, to our own local rules.

What people need is money. They migrate because they do not have any money. So we're putting in irrigation. It is no good looking at the sky and hoping it will rain. People leave the community because there is no way to make a living. Rather than eradicate coca, why doesn't the government spend the money here and stop people migrating to the Chapare?

Here the sindicato *is the main form of community organisation. The municipality and the* sindicato *work hand in hand. There's no difference between us. At the same time, we are all Aymaras, we're all* originarios. *Our culture is under attack. What we ask for is respect. We want to be dealt with on equal terms. If they have cars, well why shouldn't we? This makes us angry. Felipe Quispe has done a lot to help us win better treatment. We are not animals here for other people to use. We want more autonomy, but we do not want to be independent. Our forefathers fought in the Chaco War. We are Bolivians.*

Educational reforms initiated under President Jaime Paz Zamora but implemented under Sánchez de Lozada improved school provision in the rural Altiplano. Education is widely perceived as one of the main routes to upward social mobility, and is highly valued. One of the central objectives of the reform was to promote bilingual education, in this case schooling in Aymara. Although the provision of bilingual education has encountered many problems, such as a shortage of bilingual teachers and the lack of teaching materials in indigenous languages, it seems to have had an important effect in increasing the cultural self-esteem of Aymara people in rural areas. However, it is difficult to provide secondary teaching in indigenous languages, and many question its relevance for improving access to the job market when Spanish is the language of the city.

Katarismo and the Quispe phenomenon

Ethnicity has always played a role in the politics of rural communities of the Altiplano, and there has been a long tradition of rebellion, first against colonial rule and then against the various governments of the post-independence period. As Xavier Albó, the anthropologist and Jesuit priest, has underlined, it is absurd to talk of ethnicity and peasant politics in Bolivia as if they were in separate categories; the overwhelming majority of the rural population is indigenous in terms of its identity and cultural traditions and *campesino* in occupational terms. The term *campesino* gained currency in Bolivia in the wake of the 1952 revolution, as the term *indio* was one of abuse. Post-revolutionary political discourse therefore referred to *campesinos,* although in recent years *indigenista* identities have come to the fore, partly as a way to distance today's peasant politics from those of the period of MNR pre-eminence in the 1950s and 1960s.

The first sign of the resurfacing of *indigenista* politics was the emergence of the Katarista movement, and especially the formation of the *Movimiento Revolucionario Tupaj Katari* (MRTK) in 1978. The Kataristas took their name from the late 18th century rebellion of Julián Apaza, who subsequently came to be called Tupaj Katari. Following the earlier uprisings of Tomás Katari and José Gabriel Condorcanqui (better known as Tupac Amaru), Apaza's rebellion spread throughout the Altiplano and culminated in a lengthy siege of the city of La Paz. In 1781, like Tupac Amaru before him, Tupaj Katari was hung, drawn and quartered by the Spanish authorities. The Kataristas in the late 1970s embodied two currents: the smaller *Movimiento Indio*

Tupaj Katari (MITKA) took a strongly *indigenista* line, while the MRTK took a more class-oriented stance and helped found the CSUTCB in 1979. The CSUTCB specifically rejected the collaborationist positions adopted by previous peasant union confederations. In the ten years that followed, the CSUTCB consolidated its position as the true national representative of the peasantry at the national level, although dominated politically by voices from the Aymara-speaking Altiplano.

The Katarista movement helped bring ethnic concerns closer to the centre of the political stage, as well as contributing to a critique of the previous pattern of agricultural development in Bolivia. As a leading participant in the COB, the CSUTCB reflected the basically *sindicalista* orientation of the Bolivian labour movement as a whole, but it helped bring into focus a more specifically *indigenista* agenda. This was given added force in 1992 by the 500th anniversary of Columbus' voyage to the Americas, which helped sensitise NGOs and other funding agencies to the plight of indigenous communities in the region. During the 1980s, however, the Katarista movement splintered into a number of factions. One of these, the *Movimiento Revolucionario Tupaj Katari de Liberación* saw its leader, Víctor Hugo Cárdenas, become vice-president in the first Sánchez de Lozada government. The first ever indigenous Bolivian to occupy such a lofty position, Cárdenas played an important role in developing the educational and decentralisation policies mentioned above.

By 1990 the leadership of the CSUTCB had been seized by the largely Quechua-speaking *campesinos* from Cochabamba, where the *cocaleros* of the Chapare had built up a strong local *sindicato*-based organisation. Numerically, Quechua-speakers outnumber Aymaras, but Aymaras, with their strong sense of community, have taken the lead in indigenous politics. The figure of Felipe Quispe only emerged on the national stage in 1998, when he was chosen as leader of the CSUTCB to break the impasse in a fight for power between two *Cochabambino* rivals, Evo Morales and Alejo Véliz. In the early 1980s, Quispe had been involved in MITKA before he subsequently moved on to form a guerrilla-type movement, the *Ejército Guerrillero Tupaj Katari* (Tupaj Katari Guerrilla Army; EGTK). The EGTK never prospered, and Quispe spent much of the early 1990s in jail. His assumption of the title 'El Mallku' dates from the time when he was elected CSUTCB general secretary.

Between 1998 and 2001, Quispe became a major protagonist in a number of protests against the Banzer government's economic policies, spearheading *bloqueos* and other forms of protest on roads across the Altiplano. In 2000, there were two particularly important mobilisations: the first in April (at the same time as the Cochabamba water wars) and the second in October, which coincided with a teachers' strike and protests in the Chapare against the Banzer government's drug eradication activities. The second extracted substantial concessions from an embattled government, concerned that road blocks in the Altiplano could lead to serious food and fuel shortages in La Paz. Quispe's demands were an eclectic mix of the very broad and the very specific. On the one hand he insisted on the repeal of fundamental laws, such as the INRA Law and law 21060, the 1985 decree that underpinned the stabilisation package and subsequent economic liberalisation. At the same time, he picked up on detailed points, like the provision of Altiplano peasants with new tractors. In 2000, Banzer promised to revise the INRA Law as well as a controversial forestry law, and to use HIPC funds to build peasant markets. But little was done; nine months later in June 2001, Quispe launched a fresh offensive of blockades across the Altiplano, arguing that the government had simply ignored its earlier promises. As time went by Quispe's list of demands grew.

Quispe's discourse has always been much more ethnically oriented than that of either Morales or Véliz, constantly attacking Bolivia's 'white' – read *mestizo* – elite and calling for the construction of an independent Aymara state. Morales and

Véliz, who distrusted Quispe's personal ambitions, focused more on the nefarious collaboration between La Paz and Washington in pursuit of coca eradication. *Campesino* leaders do not necessarily have a common agenda; there have been several instances when rival sectors within the CSUTCB failed to support one another in their attempts to mobilise protest. More often than not, Quispe and Morales acted alone, unsupported by the other. In October 2003, for instance, at the time of the mass mobilisation in El Alto and the Altiplano against Sánchez de Lozada and his gas export plans, Morales only threw his weight behind the growing wave of protest at the last minute. Rivalries and mistrust among *campesino* leaders run deep.

Quispe's style of leadership has also been inconsistent and vacillating, shifting in tone as well as in political praxis. His demands have changed from one moment to another, his actions apparently divorced from any clear strategic plan. Calls for insurrection and armed struggle, for instance, have not precluded his involvement in electoral politics. In the 2002 elections, as leader of the MIP, he availed himself of the opportunity to win himself a seat in the Chamber of Deputies and five others for members of his party. However, within two years he had decided to resign his seat in favour returning to grass-roots politics.

An important aspect of Quispe's discourse is its appeal to a somewhat romanticised pre-Columbian past. "This is not because he rejects modernity," says Roxana Liendo, a former director of the Catholic Church-based CIPCA in La Paz, an NGO with a long track record of working in the Altiplano. "Rather it's a coded appeal for social justice and greater respect." She quotes an old Aymara adage to the effect that "the past is before us, the future is behind," meaning that the past is what you can see and which can help you guide your actions, whilst the future is impossible to see. According to Liendo's reading of Altiplano politics, Aymara peasants want to share in the benefits of modernity, whether in the form of improved agricultural technologies or acquiring cellphones or access to the Internet. "It has everything to do with the self-respect of a proud people," she says. A poignant symbol of the value attributed to modernity has been communities' persistence in demanding that the government honour its previous promises to supply them with brand-new tractors. A number of large red Fiat tractors are to be seen in various localities around Achacachi.

A resurgence in ethnicity

Modernity vies with tradition in the Aymara world view, or indeed in what is sometimes more broadly called the *cosmovisión andina*. Aymara communities are tightly integrated into the modern world in that they maintain close contact with the urban world, where they sell many of their products and where many of their kinsmen live. Aymara people, indeed, are famous for their commercial acumen. At the same time, people's concepts of welfare often go beyond western materialistic definitions of the word, and traditional beliefs in such forces as the *pachamama* (the mother earth) remain firmly embedded. So too do notions of *usos y costumbres*.

Whether people accept Quispe's discourse or not, there is little doubt that he has had a major impact on helping build up a greater sense of self-respect and assertiveness among a people who believe they are second (if not third) class citizens in today's Bolivia. Such feelings are not just limited to rural areas, and Quispe has had an important influence among urban people, particularly the disenchanted young in El Alto. The strident and sometime violent tone of Quispe's language also finds an echo among people fed up with corrupt officials, self-satisfied NGO representatives, and even churchmen who do less than they promise to tackle poverty and marginalisation.

Recent years have seen a revaluation of the role of traditional institutions in the Aymara world. Whereas since 1952 the traditional community institution has been the *sindicato*, in some parts of highland Bolivia communities are reverting towards the *ayllu*. Where this is the case, the *ayllu* has become the institution that monitors the activities of the municipality. With their accent on defence of territory, *ayllus* are often to be found in more remote locations. However, in the vicinity of Lake Titicaca, quite close to La Paz, there have been moves to replace *sindicatos* with *ayllus*. The lead has been taken by communities like Jesús de Machaca, where there is a strong history of traditionalism.

The re-creation of *ayllus* has meant substituting posts in the *sindicato* with more time-honoured equivalents such as *mallkus*. For instance, the *secretario de justicia* becomes known as the *jallja mallku,* whose job still includes resolving disputes between individuals in the community – *jallja* means the person who decides or exercises judgement. It has become common for these *mallkus* to wear a uniform or carry insignia of their rank, including a hat (*sombrero*), whip (*chicote*), poncho and *chuspa* (a bag used for carrying coca). These symbols form part of the *usos y costumbres* which define community identity. They are used particularly on formal occasions within the community or when the authorities are called upon to represent it in the outside world. It would not normally have been the case that the authorities of the *sindicato* would have dressed up like this. The use of traditional dress, people believe, adds to the stature of their leaders. This shift towards more traditional forms of organisation in the Altiplano (though by no means everywhere) was underscored by the establishment in November 1997 of the *Consejo Nacional de Markas y Ayllus de Qollasuyo* (CONAMAQ), a challenge to the hegemony of the CSUTCB. Like the *ayllu* it represents, CONAMAQ's chief focus is on guaranteeing territorial rights.

Voices: Peasant leaders

Saturnino Tola is a deputy for the MIP. He comes from the community of Jesús de Machaca, an Altiplano community which has brought back traditional *usos y costumbres*.

The sindicato *is not a native institution, and it has made people forget the* ayllu *and the* marka. *It has weakened the observance of* usos y costumbres. *Because of machismo, this has been to the disadvantage of women especially. As* dirigentes *we have been attentive the problems of the peasantry, but at the expense of everyday things, of people's lives. The* Mallku *takes care of the members of the community, of families, and as he visits outlying farms he gives advice to fathers and sons. With the* sindicato *this was lost, at least in part. The sindicato at its various levels –* sub-central, central – *did not care for everyday concerns. It was a copy of the trade union. It did not look after the* aynoqas *(community lands worked collectively). The land was divided up and everyone did what they wanted. Production suffered, and diseases in plants and animals became more frequent. With the return of traditional authorities, we've once again resorted to the* aynoqas.

Paulino Guarachi is a former general secretary of the CSUTCB. He comes from Guaqui, a small port on the shores of Lake Titicaca.

*We have had conflicts with neighbouring communities. Guaqui is next door to Jesús de Machaca, which defines itself as an indigenous community (*comunidad originaria*). They wanted to become a* Territorio Comunitario de Origen, *and applied for* saneamiento. *This meant defining community boundaries. We had a fierce battle to defend our lands. We took the whole community out to defend our boundary. In the end, we lost a little bit of land in the negotiation that followed.*

In Guaqui, we have always had a peasant union-based local organisation, but under the influence of Jesús de Machaca it has become more indigenous. Each community now has a mallku *and* q'amanis. *But this is more a change of words than substance. The post is basically the same. The older members of the community who remember the* hacienda *days prefer the term* mallku. *They think it will win the community more respect. They now wear special clothes.*

Felipe Quispe came on the scene with very radical sounding words. He referred to the Ley INRA as a ley maldita *(the damned law). He said that its purpose was simply to raise taxation. This sort of speech found an echo among the* mallkus. *But many also see him as a threat to their social advancement. Had I been in Quispe's shoes, I would have focused more on the issue of land distribution. He tends to forget the issues that are most important to people. He says that all these everyday problems will be resolved the day we win power. For many, Evo Morales is a better bet. People are quite pragmatic in their politics; they tend to go for winners.*

The increased profile of the traditional *ayllu* has been paralleled by the increased use of customary law. Although the use of customary law (*derecho consuetudinario*) is contemplated in the most recent version of the constitution, it is often unclear what the precise frontiers are at the community level between the formal judicial system and customary law. This can lead to conflicts of authority. One common problem area is the rules governing the inheritance of property. Usually, customary law applies solely to matters that are internal to the community, and the sort of punishments that can be inflicted on culprits are limited. In most places, the most extreme form of punishment is the banishing of a person from the community. Such punishments as the lynching of public authorities – as occurred in the town of Ayo Ayo in 2004 – do not form part of customary law.

Successful mobilisation requires coordination, especially synchronisation in the mounting of road blocks. However, this is not always easy to achieve, and peasant leaders in different parts of the Altiplano frequently are reluctant to cooperate with one another. Communities may not wish to take such extreme measures which may clash with other local priorities. *Bloqueos* can often lead to pitched battles with the police or army in which people are killed or wounded. They also interrupt commercial activities and can cause frictions with those whose livelihoods depend on the transport or sale of agricultural products in urban areas. There has to be regard to the agricultural calendar; people are unwilling to abandon their fields during times of sowing and harvest. Normally such measures are a last resort; custom dictates that measures of force are only used once other preliminaries, such as dialogue or verbal threats, appear to be going nowhere. Usually, the first steps towards negotiation take place under the auspices of the local municipality. However, patience has run thin in recent years, and the good faith of the authorities in responding to community demands has increasingly been called into question as promises are never properly fulfilled. Consequently, communities have increasingly resorted to blocking roads as a way of drawing public attention to their demands. The *bloqueo* is a community decision and once adopted it will usually be carried out by all in disciplined fashion. Until the road is blocked, it often seems, no-one in authority takes much notice. Disputes develop into confrontation quickly as trust diminishes.

A view from the other side of the lake

Although the majority of Aymaras live in Bolivia, probably a third live across the other side of Lake Titicaca in Puno, Peru. There are also Aymaras who live in northern Chile. In ethnic terms, the frontiers between the three countries are arbitrary dividing lines that came into being when Bolivia, formerly Alto Peru, split off to become a separate nation in 1825. Aymara communities in Peru share many of the same characteristics of their Bolivian equivalents. However, Aymara nationalism is essentially a Bolivian phenomenon. Felipe Quispe is not given much attention in Puno – still less in Chile – nor has he sought to create a following there. Meetings have been held about establishing Collasuyo with people from Peru, but this has never amounted to much.

In Peru, *indigenismo* has played much less of a role in rural politics than in either Bolivia or Ecuador. The reasons for this are a source of controversy among historians and anthropologists. In part it was because the agrarian reform, which took place later in Peru than Bolivia, broke with the notion of *indigenismo.* As in Bolivia in the 1950s, it abolished the remnants of serfdom, raised the status of the *campesino* and opened up new paths towards 'modernity' and 'citizenship'. The history of the left in Peru is also rather different to that of Bolivia. José Carlos Mariátegui, the founding father of Peruvian Marxism, effectively reinterpreted *indigenismo* as an expression of class struggle, not of ethnic division. Most of those on the left active in rural politics have followed the ideas set out by Mariátegui; even the official title of Shining Path (*Sendero Luminoso*), the Maoist-inspired guerrilla organisation that decalred war on the state in rural Peru in the 1980s, was 'Por el Sendero Luminoso de José Carlos Mariátegui'. Much more so than in Bolivia, peasant unions in Peru have tended to be controlled by parties of the left, and the Peruvian left has chosen to organise along class rather than ethnic lines.

The politics of Puno, the area of Peru where most Aymaran people live, have been shaped by the legacy of the agrarian reform since the 1970s. It has been largely a struggle for land, since many of the indigenous communities, both Quechua-speaking and Aymara, were bypassed by the reform which concentrated the lands of former *haciendas* in large-scale units run by former *hacienda* employees. The Peruvian Peasant Confederation (*Confederación Campesina del Perú*; CCP), strongly *Mariateguista* in orientation, spearheaded the occupation of land in Puno, demanding the restructuring of the agrarian reform. Indigenous communities, at the same time, found themselves confronted by Sendero Luminoso and its uncompromising Maoist ideology. Aymara communities, with their tight local community organisation, fared much better than their Quechua neighbours in resisting the inroads of Sendero. They were not prepared to accept Sendero Luminoso demands that they cut commercial relations with the outside world and revert to subsistence farming. For this reason, as well as for reasons of political culture, it is hard to imagine an organisation like Sendero gaining a strong foothold in Bolivia, even though Sendero sought refuge there. The lynching of a mayor in the Peruvian town of Ilave, near to Lake Titicaca, in April 2004, awakened fears in Lima that the *indigenista* spirit was indeed spreading across the frontier. However, this incident appears to have had more to do with vendettas among former Peruvian Maoists and a reaction against mayoral arrogance than any sort of ethnically-inspired uprising.

Though the *wiphala* (the flag of *indigenista* identity) is occasionally to be seen in rural Puno, the joining in the creation of the Aymara nation shows few signs of becoming a major priority for those living on the other side of the lake.

6
El Alto and the 'Gas War'

The burnt-out shell of what used to be the municipal buildings in the centre of El Alto is a poignant reminder of the social conflicts that shook this city of the poor in 2003. As if to reinforce the point, a billboard across the main highway and pointing towards the city hall says 'Courtesy of the IMF'. The city hall was a casualty of the violence that occurred in February 2003, when the Sánchez de Lozada government almost fell after a police strike led to rioting both in La Paz and in El Alto. Businesses were looted and the headquarters of political parties assaulted. One victim of looting was the Caja de Los Andes savings bank, around the corner from the El Alto municipality. Today, it is better protected, with sturdy grilles installed over all the windows. Some in El Alto even believe that it was the mayor himself who burned down the municipality, since such a thorough job was made of destroying all the documentation it contained about municipal finances and business contracts.

No such monuments are required to remind people of the events that took place only eight months later in October 2003, when days of public protests throughout El Alto finally brought the government of Sánchez de Lozada to its knees, at a cost of 70 dead and 200 wounded. This was a pivotal moment both in the recent history of El Alto and indeed in that of Bolivia itself, when ordinary people took matters into their own hands and forced their rulers to heed their demands. The citizens of El Alto proved to themselves and others that they had political muscle.

City of the poor

Thirty years ago, La Paz's international airport stood on the edge of El Alto, adjacent to the headquarters of Bolivia's modest air force. Today, the airport and the air base are right in the centre of the city, surrounded by many kilometres of sprawling suburbs. This is Bolivia's (and one of Latin America's) fastest growing urban areas, with an annual estimated population growth rate of over 5%. With a population approaching 750,000, nearly one in ten Bolivians is a resident of El Alto, and within a few years its population will exceed that of La Paz itself.

El Alto is situated on the edge of the Altiplano, where it suddenly gives way to the steep-sided crater in which Bolivia's seat of government (the capital of Bolivia is still theoretically in Sucre) is situated. Wherever you are, the snowy peaks of the Andes look down: Huayna Potosí, Chacaltaya, Mururata and, most majestic of all, Illimani. Whereas in many Latin American cities the wealthiest neighbourhoods are situated higher up than the poor districts because the air is better, the reverse is true in La Paz. At 3,800 metres above sea level, the most prosperous districts are at the lowest altitudes where temperatures are a few degrees warmer. El Alto, as the name implies, is well above the rest of the city. The air is thinner and there is nothing to break the cold winds as they blow across the flat Altiplano. As a signpost proclaims as you reach the rim of the crater travelling up the motorway up from La Paz, 'welcome to El Alto, the world's highest city where God watches us closest up.'

Over the years, La Ceja (literally, 'the brow') of El Alto has emerged into a district of frenetic commercial activity, a hub for the buying and selling of goods from all over the Altiplano and beyond. The trading area now spreads out into neighbouring districts. The drivers of taxis and minibuses at La Ceja vie with one another for passengers either descending to La Paz and its more moneyed suburbs below, or setting out on longer journeys across the Altiplano. There are three main axes that radiate out from La Ceja: the main road to Oruro and the south of Bolivia (the Avenida 6 de Marzo); the road westwards to Lake Titicaca and beyond it to Peru (the Avenida Juan Pablo II); and between them the road to Viacha (the optimistically-named Avenida Hacia el Mar, the Road to the Sea). Between these three axes, large urban neighbourhoods have grown up, peopled mainly from other parts of highland Bolivia but especially the surrounding Altiplano.

El Alto has become, in effect, the Aymara capital. There are many whose families have lived here for three generations or more, but it is essentially a township of rural migrants. Although some have managed to climb the social ladder and achieve relative wealth and esteem in their communities, the vast majority of people are poor and are likely to remain that way. Well-paid jobs are scarce and industrial development in El Alto has failed to keep pace with the rapidly rising population. Most people struggle to make a living in low-paid commercial activities or service industries in the so-called informal sector. Housing conditions are poor and overcrowded, and those living in the cheaper outskirts of the city (where basic services are often lacking) find themselves with long journeys into work in and around La Ceja or even further if they work down in La Paz itself. The architecture of El Alto rarely rises above the functional, a mélange of red brick, reinforced concrete and corrugated iron. But occasionally, when money allows, buildings bloom into more exotic garb, adorned with stucco, brightly coloured tiles and coloured glass. In particular, El Alto baroque with its onion domes and *campanile* makes the city's many churches stand out as esoteric landmarks in an otherwise drab urban townscape.

Movers and shakers

The various neighbourhoods of El Alto form close-knit and community-conscious units. Much of this organisational tradition comes from rural communities of the Altiplano, of which the large majority of residents are descendants and with whom they maintain frequent and close contact. Also important has been the influx of ex-miners and other unionised workers who acquired cheap housing through the *cajas*. According to Alfredo Cahuaya, who works with children's projects in El Alto, the city shows how rural cultural values persist in an urban setting. He notes that there is a clash between traditional ways of doing things and the challenges of urban life, but that "the idea of the community persists, and with it a degree of control over elected leaders." There is a strong sense of accountability among community leaders towards their grass-roots, which has the effect of strengthening local groups. "If they don't behave in the way people want, they get turfed out of the positions to which they are elected," he says. "This is a very democratic city."

Probably the most important social actors in El Alto are the neighbourhood committees (*juntas vecinales*), which are represented at the city level by the Federation of Neighbourhood Committees (*Federación de Juntas Vecinales* or Fejuve). The Fejuve represents 570 *juntas vecinales* in all of the eight districts into which El Alto is divided. The *juntas* have a long history of collective action, built on the attempts of individual neighbourhoods to access municipal services (such as electricity and water) as well as in the construction of basic neighbourhood infrastructure like roads and street lighting. It is worth noting that the term *vecino* can mean both 'neighbour' and 'citizen'. Under the Popular Participation Law, the neighbourhood committees were called upon to oversee the activities of the municipality and the distribution of municipal funding. This gave them a powerful role that often pitted them against the mayor and municipal authorities. Well before the gas war the Fejuve played an important part not just in campaigning for public works to be carried out, but in criticising the mayor, questioning the efficacy of the local authorities, and resisting attempts to raise thresholds of local taxation.

Four other types of organisation played important roles in helping organise protests in El Alto in 2003. The *Central Obrera Regional* (Regional Workers' Confederation; COR), a local branch of the COB, emerged as an important actor. Although the COR is largely composed of commercial traders of one sort or another, it also involves unionised factory workers. The *sindicato* is an important institution, even among informal sector workers. Secondly, there was the Women's Federation (*Federación de Mujeres*). Thirdly, there were the former mineworkers living in El Alto with their esprit de corps and organisational experience. Finally, students, who – centred on the University of El Alto – adopted a particularly radical tone in local political activity. In practice, these organisations were not mutually exclusive, and many people were involved in two or even more at the same time. The demonstrations that took place in October 2003 involved large numbers of people, and though the dynamic of events was fast-moving and fairly spontaneous, they would not have happened in this way if they had not been based on a bedrock of strong social organisation.

In party political terms, El Alto has seen a variety of different movements gain prominence within the local municipality, but there has been much less coherence at this level. The late 1980s and 1990s saw the rise of *Conciencia de Patria* (Condepa), a populist party founded and led by 'Compadre' Carlos Palenque, a well-known media figure. Condepa started off as a counterpoint to the traditional parties, but ended up largely co-opted by them. After Palenque's untimely death, the reins of the party were taken over by his wife, Mónica Medina. Condepa appealed specifically to the urban Aymara voter, and the party had less electoral success in the rural sphere. In the late 1990s, Condepa's shoes were partly filled by José Luis Paredes of the MIR, who won the municipal elections of 1999 and was re-elected as an independent in 2004. Populism has played an important role in local *alteño* politics alongside wide fluctuations in party loyalties. An increase in support for Evo Morales and the MAS, who received more votes than any other candidate in El Alto in the 2002 presidential elections, was partly reversed in 2004 when the MAS came second.

As elsewhere in Bolivia, politics in El Alto runs along two tracks that do not necessarily lead in the same direction: mobilisational politics and electoral politics. The widely fluctuating electoral support for parties and their leaders suggests that political loyalties are fickle. In El Alto, as in the rest of Bolivia, most people are heartily fed up with political parties, even popular-based ones like the MAS. Party leaders are seen as unresponsive to the interests of those who vote for them. Until 2004, there was no alternative but to vote for political parties, since legally all candidates for elective office had to run under the label of a registered party. The scrapping of this restriction promised to give greater voice to civic groupings, but these only made modest headway in the 2004 municipal elections.

The gas factor

The discovery of large reserves of natural gas in the south-eastern department of Tarija in the late 1990s had far-reaching implications for the direction that the country's future economic development path would take. It would also inject some new elements into its politics.

While the tally of total reserves of natural gas totalled 5.7 trillion cubic feet in 1997, by the end of 1999 it had reached 23.7 trillion cubic feet. By October 2001, it stood at 47 trillion cubic feet. Bolivia's gas reserves were second only to those of Venezuela in the Western Hemisphere. With this sort of hydrocarbons potential, attention swiftly moved to how Bolivia could use the resources to boost exports.

In July 2001, a consortium of oil and gas companies – led by Spain's Repsol but also involving BP-Amoco and British Gas – came up with a scheme to use Bolivian gas to help meet the energy deficit on the western seaboard of the United States. The gas would be piped from Tarija across the Andes to the Pacific, whereupon it would be liquefied and then shipped to northern Mexico. There it would be turned back into gas and pumped through a pipeline across the border into California.

The scheme raised immediate questions over the route that the Pacific pipeline would take. The quickest and cheapest option was to use a Chilean port as the point of liquefaction and shipment. The other option was the Peruvian port of Ilo. The consortium made clear its preference for the former. Not only would the Chilean pipeline be shorter and therefore cheaper, but it considered that Chile's lower country risk made investing there much more attractive (and more economical) than Peru.

This raised immediate problems, first for the Quiroga government (2001-02) and thereafter for Sánchez de Lozada. Both presidents intimated support for the Chilean option, but were aware that making the country's future exports dependent on Chile would be a difficult sell to public opinion in Bolivia. It was Chile which, in the War of the Pacific (1879-83), had rendered Bolivia landlocked by capturing its maritime province of Antofagasta. As every Bolivian schoolchild knows, recovery of the lost department is a duty, and the country's armed forces have long seen this as their mission. In the words of Mercedes Condori, a Fejuve executive member in El Alto, "we were brought up on the idea of rancour towards Chile because they stole our territory; we educate our children in the same way." Working out some mutually acceptable compromise has proved impossible, and the accusation of 'selling the country short' has long been a potential political death knell for Bolivian presidents. Because of these and other disputes, Bolivia and Chile have not had full diplomatic relations since 1978, the only two countries in the Americas to permanently spurn such ties.

With the Repsol/BP/BG consortium firmly committed to the Chilean option, and the potential US purchaser of Bolivian gas increasingly pushing for a decision, Sánchez de Lozada found himself on the horns of an uncomfortable dilemma by the end of 2002. Domestic opposition within Bolivia to the whole gas sale project was becoming more vocal, and as the government's popularity diminished the campaign on the gas issue gained momentum. The government resisted suggestions that the issue be put to a referendum because it knew that such a referendum would be well-nigh impossible to win. At the same time, it showed little enthusiasm for investigating the alternative scheme to ship gas through Peru. It appeared wedded to the Repsol plan, yet unable to say so publicly.

One of the issues that came to the surface during the gas war was the demand that gas be used first and foremost for domestic industrialisation purposes. It as argued by some that this would help the country's development, help to resolve chronic unemployment problems and, eventually, lead to the export of products with a higher value-added than raw materials. Alternative uses of natural gas did not appear to loom large in the plans of Sánchez de Lozada or the consortium.

Voices: The *Comité de Vigilancia*

Eusebio Merlo is a member of the *Comité de Vigilancia* in his neighbourhood of El Alto.

We reflect a lot on our history. Look what they did to the Cerro Rico (the silver deposit in Potosí that supplied Spain with half the silver it acquired from its colonies in the Americas). *Our history is one of* saqueo *(plunder) and we are left begging in the streets. We look at what happened to our ancestors, and now we see history repeating itself. What are our children going to live off? This is why we think the industrialisation of gas is so important.*

The gas and other 'wars': a regime in crisis

The first clear sign that the Sánchez de Lozada government was in deep trouble was the February 2003 riots in La Paz, El Alto and other cities. The immediate cause of these was the announcement of government plans to introduce an income tax. Facing a fiscal deficit of around 9% of GDP, Sánchez de Lozada and his ministers needed to raise tax income, and believed that bringing in an income tax was politically more palatable than raising fuel prices. At this point, the government had not considered changing the contractual tax obligations of foreign investors in the oil and gas industry, although it had been looking at ways to tighten up on tax contributions. No sooner than the administration had announced its income tax measures, known as the *impuestazo*, than members of the police force used the situation to protest about their own grievances. In the chaotic events that followed, which began with a shoot-out between army troops and police in the main square of La Paz, public buildings were burned, the headquarters of political parties ransacked and business premises looted.

Claiming that he had been the victim of an assassination plot, Sánchez de Lozada managed to cling on to power, although subsequently he sought to defuse tensions by reshuffling his cabinet and rescinding the tax plan. He appealed instead to the IMF for greater leniency in meeting fiscal targets. The response of people living in El Alto and elsewhere to the *impuestazo* had been immediate. They saw this as simply one more economic burden being arbitrarily placed on the shoulders of those least able to pay. As far as the public was concerned, the government's about-turn on the *impuestazo* was held up as a vindication of popular protest. It set a precedent for what was to follow later in September and October.

In the build-up to the events of October, there were a number of important but separate preliminary skirmishes. The first of these took place in El Alto, and involved implementation of a plan by Paredes, the mayor, to reform the ways in which local taxes were levied. The introduction of two new local tax forms known as *'maya'* and *'paya'* – *maya* means one in Aymara and *paya* two – brought in a new system under which people would have to provide more details about the size of their properties.

While the municipality saw this as simply an administrative measure, most others saw it as a veiled device to raise municipal taxes further. The *juntas vecinales* mobilised against the *maya* and *paya,* eventually forcing the embattled mayor to back down.

The second skirmish took place on the Altiplano, where Quispe and his followers took advantage of the government's weakness to push ahead with their long list of demands. When a number of tourists found themselves trapped by road blocks in the town of Sorata, unable to return to La Paz by road, troops intervened with force. At Warisata, just outside Achacachi, troops clashed with peasants. In the words of Silvia Cosme, whose father Juan was killed that day, the troops "wanted to dismantle the road blocks, but the people of Warisata were not disposed to let this happen." In the clash that followed four *campesinos* were killed. This removed any chance of Quispe calling off the road blocks and caused fury among Aymara communities, both in the Altiplano and in El Alto. The third preliminary move was the massive demonstration that took place on September 19th in La Paz against the government's plans to export gas. Supported by the MAS and other organisations, the march saw thousands of protesters troop through the city, demanding a referendum on the country's future energy policy. The marchers also demanded the holding of a Constituent Assembly to reform Bolivia's political institutions and put an end to any future negotiations with the United States to liberalise hemispheric free trade.

In the days that followed the demonstration and the killings in Warisata, opposition to the government rapidly gained momentum. A group of mineworkers from the Caracoles mine marched on El Alto. Supported by his hard-line defence minister, Carlos Sánchez Berzaín, Sánchez de Lozada appeared to take the decision to brazen out the opposition's attempts to force his resignation, and to win what had become known as the gas war by force if need be. On October 8th, the *juntas vecinales* and the COR ordered a 'civic' strike to begin in El Alto, while Evo Morales in the Chapare announced the blocking of roads there. In the north of Santa Cruz, too, there were moves to block traffic from using the main road to Cochabamba. As the number of roadblocks around La Paz multiplied, the target of the protesters shifted from policy issues to demanding the resignation of Sánchez de Lozada and his ministers.

Thus the various different strands of public protest that had made themselves felt in previous years around the country began to come together. Attempts by the Catholic Church and the *Asemblea Permanente de Derechos Humanos* (Permanent Assembly of Human Rights; APDH) to explore possibilities for a negotiated settlement made little headway. The climax came the following week, as food and energy supplies in La Paz began to run out. When the government used force to try and bring in fuel from the Senkata refinery on the outskirts of El Alto, the stand-off entered an even more confrontational phase.

With El Alto in the hands of thousands of anti-government demonstrators on Sunday October 12th, scores of people lost their lives in confrontations with army troops. Bolivia is no stranger to political violence, but the confrontation which took place that day was more deadly than anything in recent memory. As Luis Flores, secretary for defence in his local *junta vecinal* recounts, "they tried to bring in troops from the lake (Titicaca). None of us were armed, except one or two people with sticks of dynamite. We held off the military on the bridge at Río Seco until nightfall. It was Black October: too many dead and too many wounded."

Finally, abandoned by most of his political allies (including Vice-president Carlos Mesa) and facing the possibility of a final showdown with the protesters in El Alto, Sánchez de Lozada desisted. On October 17th, he signed a letter of resignation and then fled to the United States. Mesa was sworn in as president. The US embassy swung round at the last minute to supporting Mesa as the best way to prevent further radicalisation and to maintain a cloak of constitutional continuity.

Voices: Women's organisations

For 21 years, Gregoria Apaza, an NGO, has worked with women and women's organisations in El Alto. Women have played a growing role in its community politics, especially since 2000. Clotilde Loza is in charge of community affairs.

There had been a lot of discussion in El Alto about the issue of the gas. People have come to see it as just the latest in a long line of attempts to use our natural resources for the benefit of foreign interests and not for that of ordinary people. Our resources have been squandred throughout history: silver, rubber, tin and now gas. What will people be able to leave their children and grandchildren? The MAS grew rapidly in El Alto on the back of arguments over our resources being given away at knock-down prices. There was a lot of discussion, debates and workshops about the gas issue, and people gained a great deal of information.

It started as a 24-hour protest strike about the gas, but became an indefinite action because of the violent reaction of the government. On the Saturday (October 11) it spread all over El Alto as people came out to protest in solidarity. It became a struggle against military repression. There were road blocks, trenches and all sorts of things to stop military vehicles from passing. People developed their own defence strategies, quite spontaneously. Nothing had been planned in advance.

There was strong involvement from all sectors. The men marched, and the women kept the watch. There were food shortages, so there were communal soup kitchens (ollas comunes) in each street. It was struggle of everyone. We've never seen the like in El Alto before.

The gas issue was one amongst many, but it succeeded in bringing together a very disparate and heterogenous opposition. Though triggered by the proposal to sell gas through Chile, it was a much more profound rejection of a style of government that appeared arbitrary, undemocratic and – in the final analysis – prepared to use military force to make its own agenda prevail. To many, then, the ousting of Sánchez de Lozada seemed to represent the ending of a lengthy political cycle that had begun with liberalising economic reforms in 1985 but which had led to a type of democracy in which people's interests were not taken into account. The party system that had run the country through a system of pacts since 1985 offered little by way of meaningful alternatives, whilst real decision-making seemed to be in the hands of the US embassy and the multilateral banks. At the same time, new challenges to the status quo had emerged with a forcefulness that had been largely absent since the early 1980s. In this sense, 2003 had shown that the citizens of El Alto had come of age.

The role of radio

Radio Pachamama played an important part in the protests, providing people with information. Lucia Sauma is its director.

We were the only radio to report on the 23 deaths that took place at Chasquipampa. In the days that followed, people just called the radio by cellphone and told us what was going on in their neighbourhood. In this way we ended up with hundreds of reporters all over the city. There were also loud-speakers at street corners which were tuned into us. We were thus able to direct ambulances to the wounded. Other radio stations in La Paz and elsewhere retransmitted our signal. We even had calls from Canada and France.

Sequel: the energy referendum

When he took over the reins of government from Gonzalo Sánchez de Lozada, Carlos Mesa could not just carry on as before. Among his first announcements was the decision to convene a binding referendum on the gas question. He also announced that there would be a Constituent Assembly to revise the constitution. His government, he stressed, would provide mechanisms for consultation with the public; it would not fall into the habit of ignoring public protest and resorting to military force. But he made it clear that he would not abandon the economic model he had inherited from his predecessors, nor seek to distance Bolivia from the United States. Policy making, it seemed, would have to be based on some skilful political footwork from a president who was not a professional politician, had no party to back him up in Congress, and had no organised backing in the country.

The new government's decision to push ahead with holding a referendum on the gas issue – a course of action finally accepted by Sánchez de Lozada in his last few days in office and under overwhelming pressure – involved obvious risks. Would not the people vote overwhelmingly to reject a proposition to export gas, especially if it meant piping it through Chile? Was this not the very issue over which some seventy people had been gunned down in El Alto? And wouldn't a referendum further deepen regional tensions with the eastern part of the country where Bolivia's hydrocarbons reserves are located and where opinion favoured the export project?

The advantage of a referendum was that it would give the new president, who enjoyed strong initial popularity, a decisive role in the framing of the questions to be put to voters. The course adopted by Mesa was to take the controversial issue of gas exports and to blend it in with a number of other pending energy issues on which it would be easier to rally public support. These included increasing the royalties to be paid by foreign oil and gas companies and reasserting the role to be played by YPFB, the still publicly-owned shell of the privatised hydrocarbons industry. They also included commitments to the industrialisation of natural gas. Furthermore, Mesa deftly linked the building of the Chilean pipeline to Bolivia's achieving progress in its objective to regain some sort of sovereign access to the Pacific Ocean.

In the end, five questions were put to voters in the referendum held on July 18th, 2004. Amid considerable confusion as to what they really meant, Mesa was able to win a striking victory achieving a substantial 'yes' majority for all five. Moreover, turnout was reasonably high, confounding those in the opposition who had called for abstention or even the destruction of ballot papers. On three of the questions – the repeal of the existing hydrocarbons tax law, the assertion of national ownership of hydrocarbons at the wellhead and the strengthening of YPFB – the 'yes' vote was well over 80%. On the two others – the use of gas to negotiate with Chile and the approval of gas exports subject to meeting local industrial demand – the margin was lower, but well over half. Alone, the MAS had campaigned for voters to support the first three points but to reject the last two. Like others after the referendum, the COB demanded full-blown re-nationalisation of the whole oil and gas sector.

While the outcome gave Mesa the authority he had been looking for to push ahead with plans to export Bolivian gas, it also pushed him into tricky negotiations with foreign companies on changing the contractual basis on which they did business in Bolivia. In redrafting the hydrocarbons law, the government hoped that the size of the country's gas reserves and export potential would entice the foreign oil and gas companies to accept its terms, avoiding the need for international litigation. The companies argued that they could not accept a violation of the existing contracts. At the same time, with Chile unwilling to cede territory under duress, the more expensive Peruvian option seemed the only viable solution. But Peru had its own gas to sell to the outside world; why would it give priority to Bolivia? Meanwhile, public opinion pushed for re-nationalisation and the re-launching of YPFB. So while Mesa had won a battle with the referendum, he was a long way from winning the war.

Conclusions

The waves of protest that swept through Bolivia in the first few years of the new millennium would have surprised observers looking at the country a decade earlier. In the mid-1990s, Bolivia had been held up by the World Bank and others as a model for how to reconcile economic liberalisation with the consolidation of democratic politics. Bolivia, it seemed, had achieved an unaccustomed political stability, underwritten by a commitment to the policies of the Washington Consensus. Ten years on, the prognosis seemed very different. The quest for some sort of workable consensus seemed much harder to achieve. Most Bolivians had become highly critical of the outcome of liberalising reforms and the politicians most closely identified with these. The politics of the street had re-emerged, indicative of the lack of faith in parliamentary institutions. Bolivia seemed to be experiencing an unresolved power struggle between those with power and money and those without. Some commentators, indeed, suggested that the country was one bent on its own self-destruction ('*un país suicida*'). Others ominously talked of Bolivia as a 'failed state', a dangerous vacuum liable to be filled by nefarious drug dealers, terrorists, or messianic populists.

The purpose of this short book has been to broach the issues of dissent and protest, beginning with the Cochabamba water war and ending with the El Alto gas war, in an endeavour to understand their causes and dynamics. It has argued that these bouts of confrontation have rational explanations which need to be understood. They are rooted in a sense of inequality, exclusion and discrimination, and in a political system that – despite some of the reforms passed – still had strong barriers (formal and informal) to genuine participation and negotiation. They are also rooted in a tradition of 'doing politics' that highlights protagonism and direct action at the margins of parliamentary procedures. This tradition may not be one of classic liberal democracy, but it is one based on the strength of collective organisations, organisations that command public support and enjoy the legitimacy of tradition in a country where communitarian politics has deep roots. Protest movements did not necessarily eschew procedures of negotiation, but sought negotiated settlements that would satisfy their demands. They were not generally violent, although they were often the victims of violence perpetrated against them. And they did not deny the validity of democratic institutions, like the Congress or local municipalities, rather they coexisted and interacted with them.

The change of government in October 2003, with Carlos Mesa replacing Gonzalo Sánchez de Lozada as president, represented an important shift, coming as it did in the wake of violent confrontation between a government and popular organisations. It emphasised the need to establish some new sort of social contract, a pact that would seek to reconcile the interests and agendas of different political actors, but one which took into account the lessons of the rising tide of protest during the previous months and years. Orchestrating such a pact was never likely to be easy, but Mesa at least embraced the idea – previously rejected – of a Constituent Assembly to reformulate the country's political system in ways that sought to better balance divergent interests.

Lacking an organised base in parliament and in the country more generally, Mesa and his government would find it difficult to drum up such a new framework for consensus, one that somehow reconciled the demands of social movements, local elites and foreign interests. How to balance the desires of the citizens of El Alto, emboldened by the gas war, with the interests of foreign oil and gas companies? How to weigh the demands of multilateral banks with those pushing for a return to a state-run economy? How to reconcile the demands of the US embassy on coca eradication with the need to cultivate political support from Evo Morales and the *cocaleros* in the Chapare? How to deal with the demands of powerful and entrenched interest groups, keen to extend their own power at the expense of a weak government, whilst at the same time seeking to create a greater sense of fairness?

Mesa, having said that he was determined to stay in office until 2007 (the end of the term for which he was constitutionally elected as vice-president in 2002), would need resourcefulness, ingenuity and a good deal of luck to stay the course. By the beginning of 2005, the country was once again paralysed by protests of different types. The citizens of El Alto were once again up in arms, protesting against IMF-required fuel price rises. *Campesinos* in the Altiplano were once again blocking roads in pursuit of unattended demands. The *Comité Pro Santa Cruz* was orchestrating strikes and occupations in its campaign for regional autonomy. The *cocaleros* were demanding the nationalisation of hydrocarbons. Unwilling to confront these by force, the government ran the risk of making humiliating concessions that further undermined its authority.

This book has drawn attention to both the limitations as well as the strengths of protest movements. Four limitations stand out:

The first is the problem of sustainability. Protest in Bolivia tends to be episodic, reaching swift showdowns after which there is a period of distension and dialogue. Both in the urban and rural spheres, protest campaigns are difficult to maintain over lengthy periods of time; they have to take into account the economic necessities of those involved. In the urban sphere, where commercial activities prevail, lengthy interruptions to the supply of goods quickly encounter resistance. Rural protest is subject to the vagaries of the agricultural calendar. In most of the instances I have looked at, protest was intermittent, not constant. The Cochabamba water war passed through various phases, not all of which involved the same intensity of action. The pensioners' march was spread over several years. In the case of the gas war in El Alto, the costs of the economic disruption it caused would sooner or later have caused a retreat if the confrontation had not led so speedily to Sánchez de Lozada's resignation.

A second characteristic is a problem of disunity. The fragmentation of social movements in Bolivia reflects the extraordinary heterogeneity of this diverse country. Instances of protest tend to be localised responses to specific problems. Demands in one part of the country differ from those in another. And no longer is there an overarching organisation, such as the COB, that can effectively coordinate pressure in different sectors. The lack of unity is evident in the leadership rivalries in organisations like the CSUTCB. Despite its name, the CSUTCB does not operate as a single national force.

Thirdly, to be successful, protests need to harness widespread public support and sympathy. We have seen how the Cochabamba water war and the El Alto gas war involved alliances that brought together different communities and actors. Such alliances are not always easy to build, and often they come about more by accident than design.

A fourth limitation is that protest movements by nature tend to be reactive. They are protests in response to perceived threats, rather than the pursuit of positive agendas. So the water war was a protest against privatisation, the mobilisation in the Chapare a protest against coca eradication, the land conflicts in Santa Cruz a reaction to the monopolisation of land. They therefore did not usually involve the genesis of workable solutions or strategies for change. In the event of becoming president, what would Evo Morales actually do?

Despite the fragmentation, however, we have also identified some important connections between these various movements; they were more than just simply the sum of their parts.

At an operational level, the timing of different protests had much to do with the opportunities created by others. This means that mobilisation tended to move in waves. Pressure on government in one place adds to the chances that pressure elsewhere would be successful. The bandwagon effect therefore involves informal coordination between different actors. And where protest movements were most successful, they tended to take place simultaneously with separate protests elsewhere, making it harder for government authorities to hold their ground. The final phase of the Cochabamba water war coincided with mobilisations in the Chapare and in the Altiplano. In 2003, it was partly the threat of protest spreading across the country as a consequence of the gas war that eventually forced Sánchez de Lozada to back down in El Alto. But such coordination was generally informal and ad hoc.

At a more ideological level, there are also some important common strands between different movements, making the outcome of one important for the development of others. All, in one way or another, were reactions against aspects of the reforms of the 1980s and 1990s – whether privatisation, the INRA law and the ending of state pensions – and the inequities and social divisions to which these gave rise. The defence of natural resources by those whose livelihoods depended on them (whether coca, water, land or gas) was another important common denominator, raising important issues of ownership and control of these resources. Respect for the traditional rights of communities, the *usos y costumbres,* against private ownership was another unifying factor, as was respect for the culture of ethnic majorities. Similarly, taxation and the use to which government revenues were put was a common factor. Who should shoulder the burden of financing the state, especially when so much public money seemed to be siphoned off in government corruption? Finally, and connected with all the foregoing, was the overbearing role played by outside actors in Bolivia: the IMF, the World Bank, the American embassy, USAID and others in the so-called international community. The Bolivian voting public might well ask whether these entities had much more direct influence over everyday government decisions than they did.

To sum up, then, protest movements were a reaction to an underlying question: who had benefited most from the way that decisions were made and the direction that events had taken over the previous two decades? These generated a widespread questioning of the practices and preferences of government, and the relationship between the state and civil society, between the rulers and the ruled. At the time of writing (March 2005), this sort of questioning was still manifest even though the Mesa administration had managed to defuse some of the tensions that brought down Sánchez de Lozada. The promise of a Constituent Assembly offered a route to build a new social compact by reforming the country's political institutions. A frank and open dialogue between social and political actors may help create confidence and new institutional devices to mediate and mitigate conflict. But successful constitutions themselves have to be built on foundations of trust and consensus; it was hard to see how these were going to be generated.

Acknowledgements

The list of people in different parts of Bolivia who gave up their time to talk to me and share their views is too long to mention everyone by name, but this book is dedicated to them. However, I would like to thank the following personally for their comments and suggestions, and for helping me arrange interviews. In alphabetical order they include: Juan José Avila, Mauricio Bacardit, Alfredo Cahuara, Ana Maria Campero, Ann Chaplin, Sonia Cuentas, Carmen Ledo, Roxana Liendo, Val Mealla, José Pimentel, Georgeann Potter, Fernando Salazar, Godofredo Sandoval, Miguel Urioste and Diego Zavaleta. I would like to thank Sam Bickersteth and his colleagues at DFID for supporting this project and agreeing to help finance a Spanish translation of this book. May I also thank the staff at Latin America Bureau for their friendly encouragement and advice. Finally, I should like to thank Judith, Suzanna and Sarah – family, travelling companions and research assistants.

Further Reading

Alvarez, N. 2003. *Provincia Velasco: El derecho a la tierra en la Chiqui-tanía*. La Paz/Santa Cruz: Fundación Tierra.

Assies, W and T. Salman *Crisis in Bolivia: The Elections of 2002 and their Aftermath*. London: ILAS (research papers).

Crabtree, J. and L. Whitehead (eds). 2001. *Towards Democratic Viability: the Bolivian Experience*. Basingstoke: Palgrave.

Gómez, L. 2004. *El Alto de pie: una insurección aymara en Bolivia*. La Paz: HdP, Comuna and Indymedia.

Dunkerley, J. 1984. *Rebellion in the Veins*. London: Verso.

Lehman, K. 1999. *Bolivia and the United States: a Limited Partner-ship*. Athens: University of Georgia Press.

Lopez Levy, M. 2001. *Bolivia: A Country Profile*. Oxford: Oxfam Pub-lishing.

Peredo, C. et. al. 2004. *Los regantes de Cochabamba en la Guerra del Agua*. Cochabamba: CESU/UMSS.

Sieder, R (ed). 2002. *Multiculturalism in Latin America: Indigenous Rights, Diversity and Democracy*. London: Institute for Latin American Studies.

Ticona, E. et. al. *Votos y wiphalas: campesinos y pueblos originarios en democracia*. La Paz: Fundación Milenio, CIPCA.

Toranzo, C et. al. 1999. *Bolivia en el siglo XX: la formación de la Bolivia contemporánea*. La Paz: Harvard Club de Bolivia.

Van Cott, D. 2003. 'From Exclusion to Inclusion: Bolivia's 2002 Elec-tions', *Journal of Latin American Studies* Vol 35, Part 4, November.

Villanueva, A. 2004. *Pueblos indígenas y conflictos de tierras*. La Paz: Fundación Tierra.

Index